Dear
White
Leader

Dear White Leader

How to Achieve Organizational Excellence through Cultural Humility

DR. JOEL PÉREZ

SENDERO
PRESS

SENDERO
PRESS

To my wife Jennifer and kids Samuel, Noah, Jayden, and Eli for being the inspiration in my life to embark on this journey and supporting me in my writing. To Mi Familia.

The Unpossessing

By Bethany Lee

The day we walked
across the unexplored island
we tore the fruit to bits
trying to locate its taxonomy
disregarding its sweetness

A generation ago or yesterday
we might have named it ourselves
after the one among us
who held the most power
(no matter what it was called
by those who loved it first)

How can I pare away
the piece of me
that thinks I can own
anything but my skin,
my flesh, and my core?

Contents

CHAPTER 1

Cultural Humility is The Key to Leading Exceptionally

IT WAS A HOT, SOUTHERN California day in May 1992, and I was meeting with other student leaders on my college campus in the lobby of my residence hall. We were scattered around the room, sitting on rundown couches with a musty smell that filled the lobby. Just a few weeks earlier, the City of Los Angeles had erupted into civil unrest after four White police officers were found not guilty of beating a Black man, Rodney King, during a routine traffic stop. What made the verdict shocking was that the beating had been recorded for the world to see. Yet the jury found the four White officers not guilty.

The outbursts of anger and violence following the verdict sent our community, state, and country into turmoil. Our campus was not immune to what was happening around us. I watched on my television set as acts of violence were committed not far from the community I grew up in. I now realize these protests stemmed from years of neglect of the financial and societal needs of those communities. I was extremely fearful of what was transpiring, because it was impacting people I knew and grew up with.

I was attending a predominantly White university where I'd started to take on a campus-wide leadership role. I had just been selected as the president of the Latino student affinity group, which I was representing at this meeting. This was a pivotal moment for those of us representing the four major cultural groups on campus at the time: Black, Korean, Latino, and White. In that meeting were members of the other ethnic clubs on campus, along with White leaders from a group whose mission was advocating for social justice issues. We wanted our university to be more inclusive of minoritized groups (LGBTQ+, racial/ethnicity, gender, disability, and so forth), so we discussed how we could create the change we wanted to see. We wanted to use the civil unrest that was happening around us to galvanize our campus and build a coalition to work together to change our campus.

In the aftermath of this monumental historical event, I began to see myself as a student leader who could bring people together who were on opposite sides of an issue. I began to see myself as a bridge builder. I didn't have the language then that I have now as a seasoned leader, coach, and diversity, equity, inclusion, and belonging (DEIB) consultant, but I was demonstrating *cultural humility*. Over the years, I have discovered that the posture of cultural humility can help leaders lead exceptionally in the areas of DEIB and navigate the complexity that comes with leading those efforts.

Thanks to my role as a campus leader, I was able to use this posture to bring campus leaders together to dialogue and work together to begin creating a sense of belonging on our campus. That experience as a student leader was the watershed moment that guided me to where I find myself today—helping individuals develop a posture of cultural humility, so they can be exceptional leaders who guide organizations to foster a deep sense of belonging.

As a campus leader, I felt scared and confused. Although I led a minoritized group, I honestly did not believe I knew how to lead in these areas. I was searching for answers and ways I could develop myself for such a tumultuous time. I did know that something needed to be done. Someone needed to provide leadership for my ethnic community on my campus. Furthermore, the work that needed to happen for our campus to become more inclusive would need all ethnic groups to work together to be successful, and this included White people.

My ethnic community could not create the change we wanted to see on our campus by ourselves. We needed to work with other people in our community. My ethnic community was looking to me for leadership—not only in my group, but the other groups on campus wanted me to be part of this movement. I knew I could not disappoint; my community, campus, and organization wanted me to be part of something that was bigger than I was. I needed to rise to the occasion if we were going to navigate the civil unrest that was happening around our country.

I needed to do something!

I was a young leader then, but what transpired during that historic event propelled me to develop my ability to lead exceptionally. It started me on my path to develop the skill set I knew was necessary to be a bridge builder.

I am now a seasoned leader who has been doing diversity, equity, inclusion, and belonging work for over thirty years. Through my extensive education and experience, I have obtained a doctorate degree, earned certificates in leading DEIB efforts, and received a lot of mentoring from DEIB leaders. I have served as a C-suite executive for an organization and have served as a chief diversity officer for another. I now serve as a consultant to organizations that want to be intentional about integrating diversity, equity, inclusion, and belonging into their ethos. My experience has also helped me be a better parent and leader in my faith community and local community.

I have mentored and coached White professionals who want to lead exceptionally in the area of DEIB. It has become crystal clear to me that no matter how much I believe I am good at this work, I still have a lot to learn. As a person of color, I continue to make mistakes along the way and sometimes offend people from different demographic or ethnic groups. However, because of my life's journey, I have developed a posture that has helped me navigate the complexities that come with wanting to be an exceptional leader in the area of inclusion, and I have taught others to do the same. To be an exceptional leader for your organization, you must develop a posture of cultural humility.

What about You?

Why did you pick up this book? Was it the catchy title, or was it because something happened in your life to shake up your worldview, like it did in mine? Was it something that happened at work?

I recently met with my longtime friend Max, who is White. He described a scenario you may be able to relate to. He traveled overseas to a leadership development program that his organization sponsored for leaders across the world who were deemed to have high potential. In a group with other participants, he noticed he was the only American. He was surprised, expecting to see more American leaders, and wondered if the program was really filled with the best and brightest or if the company was trying to meet certain diversity goals with its selection criteria.

The groups were handed a case study to work on. Max immediately thought he knew how to address the problem being described. In fact, he only saw one logical path to solving the problem. His work experience in the United States had provided him with a perspective on how to approach the situation, and he was confident his approach to the challenge would be the best approach.

Max shared his thoughts with his group. As he listened to others in his group share their proposed plans, he was surprised to find that each had a unique approach that had its own strengths. As the team collaborated, they ultimately landed on an approach that incorporated elements of most of their plans, taking the best elements from each. As he reflected on this experience, he recognized the unique perspective of each member of the group was shaped by their background and experiences, both culturally and professionally. The solution generated was more effective than any individual team member could have come up with on their own. It was at that moment he realized the value of consulting people with different perspectives before making any significant decision.

Max's perspective has changed. This experience helped him become a better leader, as he now values having people with different worldviews and cultural views around the decision-making table. He has developed a curiosity he did not have before this watershed moment.

Perhaps you are a White leader who is tired of seeing the violence that has been all too common for many minoritized groups. Now it's being made more publicly visible, and the violence is troubling you. You want to do something about this, as many of your team members are being impacted by what is happening, either personally or in their communities. They want their organization to be better; they want you to be a better leader; they are tired of not being able to show up to work as themselves; they believe they must hide their identities. You suspect this is leading to many of your best and brightest to leave your organization.

An article from *Forbes*, "These Are Reasons Your Black Employees Keep Quitting," highlights some of the reasons Black people and other members of minoritized communities leave companies and what organizations can do about it.[1] Reasons include beliefs and feelings that their workplace fosters a culture of bias and exclusionary practices, organizations do not create space for racial dialogue, and company policies and practices enable bad behavior like microaggressions to occur. Perhaps articles like this are causing you to realize that your organization needs to do something to keep this from happening.

Perhaps you are encountering differences that are challenging you to develop a different approach to leading the work of diversity, equity, inclusion, and belonging. This scenario could even be within your immediate family. Maybe a relative has disclosed to you that they identify as a member of the LGBTQ+ community, and you don't know what to do with that revelation. You have a strong desire to support them and create a space for them to explore their identity. This has created a personal challenge for you, but you know that as a family leader you need to lead exceptionally. You want to create a more inclusive community for this family member but do not know where to begin.

Maybe you are fearful of saying the wrong thing or asking questions that will lead you to being labeled a racist or bigot. You have seen what happens to colleagues when they say something wrong and how they are portrayed in the media or treated at work. You want to lead differently not only for your organization, but for your family, local community, or faith community. You want these spaces to be better, and you know it starts with you, but you don't know what to do.

I imagine one of these scenarios led you to pick up this book!

We find ourselves at a time in history that demands more of us as leaders. We cannot continue to approach the work of diversity, equity, inclusion, and belonging with the same approaches as we have in the past. Nor can we just hire someone to do the work for us. This work is complex, and the "goal posts" continue to move. This might be frustrating for some leaders, particularly if we just want to find the answer so we can move to the next organizational challenge.

If this sounds a bit like your thoughts, I can relate! I have wanted to discover an easy answer to the dilemmas that come with leading diversity, equity, inclusion, and belonging efforts so we can move on to something else. But this isn't the case.

Like you, I want to lead exceptionally. Like you, I realize this is not going to be easy. Like you, I know I need to get better. Like you, I have historically demanded more of myself. When it comes to wanting to change ourselves, our organization, and our community, we need to be exceptional leaders. Not just effective leaders.

Adopting the posture of cultural humility can help you be the exceptional leader you want to be! You will be an exceptional leader in your organization and outside of your organization in your local community and your faith community. Having a posture of cultural humility will save your organization money (less turnover), increase profits (better ideas, improved processes, increased productivity), and create employee engagement. Additionally, your life will be more fulfilling and enriched.

The Big Idea: How Cultural Humility Enhances Leadership

I'd like to talk about how cultural humility fits into organizational leadership. But first, it's important to have a clear sense of what humility looks like. When I think of the concept of humility, I think of Mother Teresa. Mother Teresa was a teacher in a school in India; all her needs were met in the convent where she lived. However, she gave up her life at the convent to live with the poorest of the poor in Calcutta, India, taking care of the sick and the dying. She took care of those no one else wanted to care for. Mother Teresa embodied the deepest form of humility.

Here is another example of humility. Recently, I attended a professional development event that included a panel discussion about how podcasting can help small business owners develop their business. In addition to sharing helpful tips, a White male panel member shared a regret regarding an oversight he had committed about the guests he had invited to participate in his podcast. He had received an email from someone who was frustrated that his podcasts did not include more people of color and women. This really shook him, as he had never given much thought to the identities his guests held; he knew this person was right. He responded by apologizing and stating that he would do better. He made a commitment to be more intentional to invite more women and people who identified as people of color to be guests. I was impressed that he shared this in the panel discussion. It demonstrated a level of vulnerability and humility. It has been my experience that when people are confronted about a bias, they immediately become defensive instead of first acknowledging that they made a mistake and apologizing.

Many of us aspire to give of ourselves for the benefit of others, yet it is very difficult to achieve. I'm sure you have heard leaders talk about how they want to remain humble in their leadership but, at times, fall short. Perhaps we can attribute this to a lack of intentional planning to develop humility. Yet as a leader, you know that approaching leadership with humility can help you become a better person, and your team will respond to your leadership example by giving of themselves for you and the organization. But where does cultural humility fit in and why?

Cultural humility has three components that when developed can help you lead exceptionally. It requires a lifelong commitment to self-awareness and self-critique (internal); redressing power imbalances in the organizations you serve, lead, or influence (external); and changing the systems to be more inclusive of all communities (systemic)[2]. (See Figure 1.)

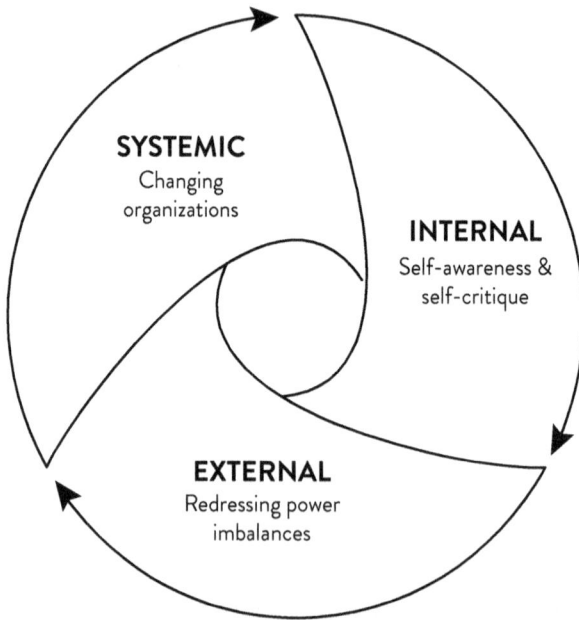

SYSTEMIC
Changing organizations

INTERNAL
Self-awareness & self-critique

EXTERNAL
Redressing power imbalances

Figure 1. Developing these three components of cultural humility will help you lead exceptionally.

When you develop these three components, you will be able to leverage cultural humility to impact your organization by creating a deep sense of belonging that will lead to higher performance and retain your talent at a higher rate. You will be able to lead exceptionally in your community, which can include your family, faith community, volunteer organizations, and wherever you serve others. The process of developing cultural humility will not be easy, nor should it be. This process requires a lot of self-work that ultimately can lead to societal change, which requires a commitment from you, the leader. Developing a posture of cultural humility will help you create the sense of belonging that many of your team members crave in your organization.

What does a sense of belonging look like? *Belonging* has become a buzzword among organizations that want to focus on decreasing their turnover rate. The *Forbes* article I mentioned earlier describes why Black and other employees of color are leaving, and you may be noticing that many of your employees may be leaving your organization because they do not feel a sense of belonging.

So, what does *belonging* mean?

The *Cambridge Dictionary* defines it as "a feeling of being happy or comfortable as part of a particular group and having a good relationship with the other members of the group because they welcome and accept you."[3] This immediately brings up images of social interaction or family, but how do we define *belonging* from an organizational standpoint? In 2019, Evan W. Carr, a behavioral scientist, and his associates in a *Harvard Business Review* article articulated what a sense of belonging looks like at work. In short, they stated that it is when team members have a sense of being accepted and included by those around them.[4]

Phyllis Weiss Haserot, a facilitator, marketing and business development strategist, speaker, podcaster, and best-selling author, challenges leaders and organizations to start developing a deep sense of belonging before addressing anything else. Organizations should encourage their people to speak up and take them seriously, encourage them to be open to curiosity and creativity, provide psychological safety, and not expect them to be perfect. Team members are welcomed, supported, and recognized for their contributions.[5]

My guess is that you are beginning to evaluate your organization to determine if it has any or all these characteristics. I ask that you don't get too far down that road, as we will address how to assess your organization in the areas of diversity, equity, inclusion, and belonging later in this book.

How to Use This Book to Lead Exceptionally

This book creates a safe space for you to learn and grow. It comprises three sections: why cultural humility is important and what it looks like (Chapters 2 and 3), how you can develop cultural humility (Chapters 4, 5, and 6), and finally its impact with concluding "take action" advice (Chapters 7 and 8). Each chapter guides you through the process of developing a posture of cultural humility and ends with exercises to help you digest what you have learned and apply it to your leadership environment.

This book begins by describing why it is imperative for you, a White leader who desires to be an exceptional leader, to start this journey. The second chapter further discusses cultural humility, so you have a clear understanding of its characteristics and what you need to do to develop it. You will begin to understand what it takes to embrace cultural humility and become an exceptional leader.

Each chapter in the second section, the how, walks you through how to develop a posture of cultural humility and provides the tools to begin the change process in yourself and your organization.

The final section, the impact, describes how developing a posture of cultural humility can impact you as an individual, your organization, and the community you are surrounded by. The book ends by describing how this work is not something to be achieved or has an endpoint, but this is a journey full of twists and turns with no endpoint.

My hope is that you will read this book cover to cover, but I know that as a busy organizational leader you might decide to skip around. It's OK to do that. You may want to go straight to the section on impact to see how the book ends. I can assure you that if you start there, you won't be able to keep from going back to the beginning to see how you can get yourself there as a leader.

As I have shared, this work has broader implications than just for you individually or your organization. It will have an impact on every aspect of your life, both personally and professionally. The great thing about this journey is that you can begin to make the changes you want to see so the areas you have influence in can change. Perhaps what you learn from reading this book will begin to initiate the change our society needs. I know this sounds a bit grandiose, but like anything that has created societal change, it starts with the individual. I know you and the people you lead want you to be an exceptional leader, so let's get started.

Take Action

➤ In the opening of this chapter, I described the watershed moment that started me on this journey. I encourage you to take five to ten minutes to identify a watershed moment for yourself. What happened in your journey that inspired you to pick up this book? Whatever it may be, take some time and write it down. This will help you lean into this experience as you begin to develop a posture of cultural humility.

➤ Take time to reflect on the characteristics that comprise a sense of belonging and note those you believe your organization exhibits. How many can you identify? Are you happy with the quality? If you are, why? If you aren't, what would it take to develop more characteristics and a deeper sense of belonging?

CHAPTER 2

Why Cultural Humility?

IT WAS A COLD AND rainy night in Los Angeles, and I was making my way through traffic to be part of a panel discussion for graduate students. These students were studying to be marriage and family therapists. The purpose of the panel was to bring people together from different points of view across the political spectrum to engage in dialogue about faith and civility. Not an easy task given the polarization that exists in our country on these two topics.

That night was also midterm elections night for our country in 2022, so our conversation was timely as there was a lot of talk leading up to Election Day around political polarization, which our country continues to be mired in. As I was driving, I tuned into election results while polls were closing around the country.

I found a parking spot and made my way across campus. The meeting room was empty and cold, as the heater had just begun to work. The chairs on the stage were set up facing the audience. Students would gather around the tables, the layout designed to facilitate discussion. I was feeling anxious and restless as I waited for my faculty colleague and fellow panelists to show up.

As I thought about the reason I was invited to speak, my fear increased. I had been asked to participate because of my moderate political views about immigration and affirmative action. I was someone whom my colleague believed could hold the middle or "straddle two perspectives." There were five other panelists. Two held more conservative views and had voted for Donald Trump in the previous election. Two held more progressive views and fell into the liberal camp when it came to politics. The final panelist, like me, held a moderate view.

The panel members also represented a diversity of ethnic groups. The two conservative panelists were a White man and an Asian woman. The two progressive panel members were a Black woman and a Latina woman. The other panelist, who was moderate, was a White woman. Although I had trepidation about participating, I knew I had the ability and temperament to engage in what was sure to be a difficult conversation.

We were asked to be prepared to discuss immigration, more specifically the policy of Deferred Action for Childhood Arrivals (DACA), and affirmative action, particularly our perspectives on both issues given our stories as leaders and members of our respective communities. As I prepared for that night, I reflected on what I could share about approaching polarizing topics using a posture of cultural humility. I decided to describe how a person can use this posture to lead exceptionally and engage in productive dialogue, which would also make the students in the audience better therapists.

The other panelists arrived, as well as my faculty colleague and her teaching partner. My face lit up as I began to see familiar faces. This helped put me at ease and get to the level of comfort I needed to engage in what would be a tense discussion. The audience began to fill the room and take their seats. We did a sound check, and then we introduced ourselves. I nervously took the microphone when it was my turn. I shared that I identified as a Mexican American son of immigrants, Spanish was my first language, and I grew up in poverty. I also shared that I had served as the interim executive director of an immigration resource center and had held several leadership roles at colleges and universities. Both areas of work directly related to the topics we were asked to address.

After our introductions, the moderator presented the first question: "What are your thoughts on DACA and the immigration challenge our country is currently facing?"

I answered the question by introducing the concept of cultural humility and how it can be helpful when having conversations that could be polarizing. I started this way because I wanted the listeners to know there is a different way of engaging in divisive topics in hopes they could learn how to do the same. I could tell that what I was sharing resonated with the audience, as they nodded in agreement. I talked about how asking open-ended questions is important, because they provide people an opportunity to share their thoughts freely without feeling as if they were being judged. I also shared about the importance of seeking to understand the other person's point of view as opposed to trying to convince the other person that your view is the correct one—a critical aspect of practicing cultural humility.

As the evening went on, we had heated exchanges, and I continued to model this approach by asking open-ended questions that demonstrated a posture of curiosity with responses like, "Say more," or "Help me understand what you mean by that." I received positive affirmation from the other panelists and from the instructors. They commented on how they appreciated my approach to difficult conversations and that they wished they could learn to take a similar approach moving forward. This was affirmation to me that this posture can work.

At one point, one of the instructors asked me directly how I felt about the topic and another panelist's statement that was anti-immigrant. She was trying to get me to directly state my position. One of the keys of using cultural humility in dialogue is to try to suspend judgment, which can be difficult, but it can be done with practice. This was my goal during the discussion, and I was able to do this, but the instructor pressed me for a direct answer.

At that point I acknowledged I vehemently disagreed with my fellow panel member. I followed up by explaining that holding a posture of cultural humility does not mean you have to abandon your values and beliefs and that, ultimately, you may agree to disagree. Using a posture of cultural humility *does* mean that you create space for difficult dialogue, so you can better understand the other person's position in a way that may cause you to change your mind. In some cases, you may change your stance, but in other cases you may not. Using a posture of cultural humility allows you to straddle two perspectives by seeing both sides of the coin. The ability to do this is central to being an exceptional leader.

Much of what I just described goes back to my early experience of campus leadership that started me on my journey toward cultural humility. This event was a manifestation of what I described in Chapter 1 when I talked about being a bridge builder. I had to demonstrate bridging polarized perspectives so I could lead exceptionally. All of this comes from a posture of cultural humility.

What Is Exceptional Leadership?

I recently had a conversation with a fellow leadership coach, Charles, about cultural humility and how it was a characteristic of being an effective leader. Charles stopped me and challenged me.

"Joel, being an effective leader should be the bare minimum when it comes to leadership."

Charles's statement implied that if you were not at least an effective leader, then you should not be leading, or at the very least you should be making every attempt to improve your leadership skills. Those words gave me pause. As I reflected on this, I could not help but agree.

By picking up this book, you are demonstrating a desire to build on applying what you have learned in becoming an effective leader to becoming an exceptional leader. You understand and demonstrate your knowledge of diversity, equity, inclusion, and belonging, and you have a strong desire to improve—personally and within your organization. Your organization needs to become more inclusive, and you're ready to take the next step to lead exceptionally: developing cultural humility.

What comes to mind when you hear someone described as an exceptional leader? You probably think of someone who can motivate the people they lead to accomplish great things. A person who can inspire and lead courageously. If you were to put "exceptional leader" into a search engine on the internet, you would find the following descriptive words: humble, courageous, authentic, self-aware, passionate, generous, accountable—all admirable qualities. But you would find it challenging to see the characteristic of cultural humility in the search results. This is because the concept of cultural humility is not familiar to leaders. This book will change that for you and those you share it with.

We are at a critical moment in our country's history that demands us as leaders (particularly White leaders) to lead in creating more inclusive organizations. If you're not sure you're ready to lead in this area, you need to do everything possible to learn how to foster a culture of belonging. If you want to lead exceptionally as a White leader who wants things to be different but do not know where to start, it begins with embodying the posture of cultural humility.

Performative Statements Don't Change Organizations

In the aftermath of the murder of George Floyd in Minneapolis in 2020, many organizations led by White leaders made promises that they would invest in the changes needed to happen within their organizations and that they would invest in Black communities. In some cases, organizations tried to follow through on the commitments they made during the Black Lives Matter movement, but many of these efforts fell short of what they promised. According to the McKinsey Institute for Black Economic Mobility, the amount promised totaled $200 billion.[6] Yet many organizations have not changed their exclusionary practices.

Lily Zheng, author of *DEI Deconstructed*,[7] does an excellent job at defining performative allyship and statements. This is when organizations make what appears to be a genuine, heartfelt statement but do not back it up with the action and resources needed to make the changes necessary to become more inclusive. This requires making the changes that lead to deep, sustainable change. Does this describe your organization?

In 2022 Dr. Shaun Harper, a *Forbes* contributor and a leading expert in diversity, equity, inclusion, and belonging, shared five possibilities as to why so many companies have not made more progress:

- Leaders may have felt compelled to make a statement but did not have a strategy to implement changes then or now, and they have focused their attention on what they perceive to be other pressing matters.

- Companies are still trying to figure out their investment strategy.

- Some companies did not plan to fulfill their commitments, figuring that the intensity of the event will diminish over time.

- Perhaps companies are spending money but on initiatives that do not include having Black team members at the table to ensure the money being spent has the greatest impact.

- Perhaps companies are doing what they said they would do but are doing a poor job at communicating their actions and results.[8]

In reviewing these possibilities, exceptional leadership is necessary to move the needle at organizations, yet it's missing in many organizations when it comes to inclusion efforts. This is where you come in!

Even after the murder of George Floyd, when people's senses were heightened about racial injustice, organizations made missteps, bringing to light the lack of exceptional leadership needed during this time. For example, in 2020 Barnes & Noble decided to celebrate Black History Month by creating what they termed "diverse custom covers."[9] These covers darkened the complexions of characters from notable works of literature, such as *Frankenstein* and *Peter Pan*. These depictions turned out to look like characters in blackface![10] (Blackface was a process where White performers in the eighteenth and nineteenth centuries would darken their skin so they could appear Black, which led to an increase in racial stereotypes.) In addition, B&N's decision not to promote Black authors over White authors during Black History Month was problematic. These decisions led to criticism, and the company canceled the promotion and later apologized for its poor decisions.

Another example of an inappropriate response to diversity, equity, inclusion, and belonging was when Walmart[11] in 2022 chose to commemorate Juneteenth by producing an ice cream flavor celebrating the holiday. Juneteenth commemorates the official ending of the Civil War on June 19, 1865. Congress made it a national holiday in 2021. Walmart was criticized for capitalizing on the holiday to increase profits without doing anything to honor the commitment to the people that the holiday celebrates. Walmart later apologized because of the intense bad press.

Where was the exceptional leadership necessary in these organizations to question the motives behind their decisions, shed light on the potential impacts and consequences, and urge a different course of action? These companies could have avoided serious public backlash if they had properly displayed cultural humility.

Our country continues to experience violence toward communities of color, ineffective performative statements continue to be issued, and organizational missteps like those by Walmart and Barnes & Noble continue to happen. What is needed to move from performative statements to action that leads to sustainable change? In 2020, Dennis Kennedy, the founder and chair of the National Diversity Council, stated, "Performative diversity, equity, and inclusion is used to convey a commitment to diversity, equity, and inclusion; however, often neglects to assign a policy, action, or person designed to bring about racial equity."[12] It takes exceptional leadership to shift an organization's mindset to focus on achieving sustainable change.

It is important to note that an exceptional leader may have the best intentions when it comes to leading their organization, but there could be an unintended, negative impact. In their book, *Did that Just Happen?! Beyond "Diversity"—Creating Sustainable and Inclusive Organizations*,[13] authors Stephanie Pinder-Amaker and Lauren Wadsworth walk readers through the steps to recover from actions that are inadvertently offensive and harmful. The first step is to apologize right away and avoid becoming defensive. You may also have to allow the other person to not respond to you after you apologize. You're giving them the agency to walk away without forgiving you or even talking about what happened. It's not about making yourself feel better. It's about making sure the other person knows you are genuinely sorry for what they experienced and that you made a mistake. This is hard, but necessary, and needs to be practiced.

Not only is it necessary to develop an individual posture of cultural humility, but that humility needs to spread throughout the organization, so the organization can effectively avoid the types of mistakes made by Walmart and Barnes & Noble. I will discuss the steps organizations need to take to develop a posture of cultural humility in Chapter 5.

It needs to be stated that the murder of George Floyd at the hands of police officers was atrocious, and it was not an isolated incident. It is another example of the abuse of power that has been happening for hundreds of years in our country. In a conversation with Leslie, a Black leadership coach, I referenced the murder of George Floyd in a way that gave Leslie the impression I believed this was an isolated case. Leslie reminded me that incidents like this have been happening for years. This atrocious incident was not new to the Black community. I immediately apologized to her with no expectation of being forgiven. The result was a meaningful conversation that left me with a better sense of how some people in the Black community feel about how the incident is portrayed as an isolated event, when it is not. You may have had a similar conversation when someone corrected your perception on this or another matter.

During President Obama's tenure, people believed his candidacy and election proved that we were living in a post-racial America. Many White people in our country held this narrative and assumed everyone could stop focusing on race, because there was no longer a need to talk about racial disparity. Yet organizational executive leadership continues to remain predominantly White and male.[14] Examples like the two I shared continue to happen, and discrimination still occurs.

In his seminal work *Stamped from the Beginning: The Definitive History of Racist Ideas in America*,[15] Ibram X. Kendi does an excellent job detailing the history of racism in our country. In reading his book, I learned that the history of racist ideas about the groups of people who lived in the Americas came from a man named Gomes Eanes de Zurara who was commissioned by King Afonso V of Portugal to write a biography of the life of the king's uncle. The writing by Zurara led to the introduction of racist ideas about Indigenous people that then took a foothold and began to spread. Before reading this, I had no idea that Zurara was the father of this idea, nor did I know anything about him. My realization has led me to think more deeply about where ideas come from, particularly those that have a harmful effect on groups of people.

Another book that impacted me was Richard Rothstein's book, *The Color of Law: A Forgotten History of How Our Government Segregated America*,[16] in which he details the history of racial residential segregation. The main takeaway from reading his work was that segregation did not happen by accident but by policies implemented by federal, state, and local governments to keep people of color from moving into communities. I had always assumed (like many others) that segregation just happened, what Rothstein refers to as *de facto segregation*.

These two books have helped me lean into curiosity to be open to a different way of thinking that veers away from what I thought I knew. If I had not developed a sense of curiosity, I would not be open to new ideas and different ways of thinking.

In reading both these books, I have come to realize that even though race is a social construct, meaning that it has been created and accepted by people in our society, it has had a devastating impact on the lived experiences of people of color in our country—experiences that cannot be explained away by just saying race should not have the impact that people say it has. People who are critical of the emphasis on diversity, equity, inclusion, and belonging efforts often promote this viewpoint, and it needs to stop.

Learning about our country's history with systemic racism is a good reminder that things continue to be the way they are because they are deeply embedded in the fabric of our nation. And unfortunately, the fabric of our nation is also deeply polarized. If I had not developed a posture of cultural humility and using curiosity to check myself, I would still hold the views that I held before reading these books. When you have developed a posture of cultural humility you, too, will be able to use curiosity to check long-held beliefs that may need to change.

Political Polarization and Creating Psychological Safety

What is political polarization? It is the divergence of political attitudes away from an unbiased center toward ideological extremes.[17] Our country is mired in it, and we have all been impacted by it in one way or another—whether it happens on social media, around kitchen tables, in places of faith, or in conversations with family members.

As polarization is firmly established in a personal context, the influence transfers to our organizations. More importantly, if you are like me, you have been told that topics of faith, race, and politics should be avoided in the workplace. The problem is that it is no longer possible to keep these topics out of our workplaces, because our colleagues have been directly impacted by these topics in one way or another—particularly those from communities being singled out in the rhetoric of the media.

In my work coaching clients from these communities, they share that they feel angry and tired. They cannot help but bring these feelings into their places of employment, and they want the freedom to talk about the driving forces of culture outside of their workplace. They have a strong desire for their organizations to say something about racial injustice and other forms of injustice that are happening around them—and impacting them. The way they feel permeates how they interact with colleagues, supervisors, and those they lead. This has a negative impact on their psychological safety, which can lead to feelings of isolation and, ultimately, a decision to leave.

What is psychological safety? Professor Amy Edmondson at the Harvard Business School defines psychological safety as "a shared belief held by members of a team that it's OK to take risks, to express their ideas and concerns, to speak up with questions, and to admit mistakes—all without fear of negative consequences."[18]

Researchers Michael Gillespie and Kaitlyn Dyshkant separate psychological safety into four quadrants: learner, challenger, collaborator, and inclusion.[19] Team members need to feel comfortable operating within these four areas:

- Learner safety—Ask questions, experiment, and learn from their mistakes.

- Challenger safety—Challenge the status quo, speak up, and express their ideas.

- Collaborator safety—Engage with each other in unconstrained ways, interact with their colleagues, and foster constructive debate.

- Inclusion safety—Know they are valued, are safe to treat all people fairly, and feel that their experiences and ideas matter.

You may be taking stock of your organization and whether it provides the types of safety that compose psychological safety for everyone in your organization. This is important work to do, and you should do it with intentionality and without relying on anecdotal evidence but on data you gather from engagement or climate studies. In Chapter 5, I will share a strategy that can help guide your efforts in leading your organization to develop the sense of belonging you desire it to have.

The people you lead want to feel safe to be who they are without fear of retribution. In a study conducted by the organization Workday, researchers found that employees want their organizations to make developing psychological safety a priority, as this is key to developing high-performing teams. The report also identified that employees believe belonging and diversity are key aspects of retaining talent.[20] People want their organizations to be inclusive and foster psychological safety, yet many organizations fall short. The challenge is intensified when there's a lack of exceptional leadership making cultural humility a priority.

You may face challenges that get in the way of leading exceptionally. Perhaps you have an underlying fear of doing the wrong thing. This fear may have paralyzed you, because you could be "canceled" for doing or saying something with good intentions but that unintentionally causes deep offense.

Cancel Culture

Many of my White coaching clients experience real fear when it comes to asking questions about how to engage in the work related to diversity, equity, inclusion, and belonging, especially of being perceived and labeled as being a bigot or racist. They have seen what happens to colleagues who are tagged with these labels and how their failures are portrayed in popular media. My clients and others need to have the freedom to ask questions and raise issues they are struggling with to find solid, workable solutions, so they can grow and become exceptional leaders.

Those struggling with cancel culture are fearful of losing their jobs. Their fear paralyzes them, keeping them from developing a posture of cultural humility. On the other hand, they also need to know that accountability may need to happen, depending on the circumstances. This is why having a coach or mentor from another cultural group can be helpful, particularly outside your organization, to find answers to your questions and help you reflect on your experiences.

As a consultant, I stress the importance of organizations creating space for risk to occur so meaningful conversations and dialogue can happen. If organizations are upfront with their leaders about addressing issues, they'll want their leaders to take risks so growth can occur.

Here are questions you might want to reflect on that will help you address any fears you may have about being labeled a bigot or racist and if you are creating space for honest dialogue to occur in your organization:

- Do you have anyone in your life with whom you can discuss diversity, equity, inclusion, and belonging? (Think about your organization, your faith community, and your neighborhood.) If not, why not?

- Can you identify several people whom you can approach with questions, so you can get answers from a variety of perspectives?

- Does your department/organization create space for people to ask questions to facilitate growth in this area?

Cultural humility can overcome cancel culture as exceptional leaders focus on creating an organizational culture that allows people to make mistakes without fear of losing their jobs. You may still need to hold team members accountable, but your organization will be stronger if you create the space to learn from mistakes. You want things to be different in your organization and community. You are seeing things from new perspectives. You are learning what it takes to be a bridge builder.

Take Action

These reflective questions will help you identify why cultural humility is needed if your organization is going to be successful in fostering a sense of belonging.

➢ After the murder of George Floyd and during the Black Lives Matter movement, many organizations made performative statements. Take time now to write down the statements your organization, or an organization you are familiar with, made after the murder. Did their statements lead to what you would consider substantive changes? Why or why not? If you did not make substantive changes, what got in the way?

➢ Sometimes we make statements with the best intentions, but they may have a negative impact. Have you ever expressed an idea that you thought was accurate, maybe even supportive, and it ended up being a misstep? Did you apologize without being defensive? What was the other person's reaction, and how did you respond?

➢ Think about your organization. Can you say with confidence that your people would say they have psychological safety as defined in this chapter?

CHAPTER 3

What Is Cultural Humility?

MY HEART WAS RACING AND I was sweating as I walked to the president's office. I was struggling as a new C-suite executive in my first year in the role. I had made a series of mistakes, causing my team to view me as ineffective and untrustworthy. I was reeling and needed to recover, as my job depended on it.

I'd had butterflies in my stomach when I received the job offer. It was a position I had dreamed of ever since I was in graduate school. I wanted to serve in a senior leadership role, so I could advocate for institutions of higher education to be more inclusive and provide a sense of belonging where students from minoritized communities could thrive. I wanted to be a mirror for students who looked like me and had a shared experience: a Mexican American, first-generation college student, and son of immigrants. I had eagerly started preparing for the role by reading books and talking with colleagues in similar roles about how to prepare for the transition. I had believed I was ready. I had even moved my family to a new state to take on this position. Now, two months into my new role, I realized I was not ready and needed help.

I knew I needed coaching to recover from the leadership mistakes I had made and rebuild the trust I had lost. As I sat down at the president's conference table, I shared with her how I believed I was ill-equipped to meet the needs of my team and could benefit from coaching. She expressed her support and encouraged me to find a coach to guide me, so I could recover from the missteps I had made during the early stages of my transition.

I found an executive leadership coach who helped me work through my approach to rebuild trust with my team and develop a stronger collaborative environment. This involved sharing with my team what led me to pursue this role, about the mentors in my life who influenced me in developing my leadership potential, and my guiding values. Being clear and transparent about my strongly held commitments helped them better understand my vision for our area of the organization and my decision-making process and leadership style. As I rebuilt their trust, I was laying a firmer foundation that I needed in order to be a successful leader.

Throughout my experience of being coached and applying valuable concepts, I realized that I, too, could help people like me build their leadership capacity to lead exceptionally and transition well into a new role. Later in my career I decided to be an executive and leadership coach and realized I needed to develop a deeper level of competency to start my journey of becoming an exceptional coach. I completed a certification program and began coaching senior leaders so I could accumulate the necessary hours to become credentialed.

As of this writing, I am now a professionally certified coach (PCC). Achieving this designation required me to develop my craft as a coach moving from competency to mastery. This is an ongoing process, because I know if I am going to continue striving to be an exceptional coach, then I will need to continue learning from others. This is the same attitude that we must adopt when it comes to developing a posture of cultural humility.

As I work with my coaching clients and present to groups, I share that when I think of the term *cultural competency*, I think of it as something each of us can achieve, a box to check, an "i" to dot, or a "t" to cross. Most people stop there, but it cannot stop there, and shouldn't stop there. Cultural competency is a milestone on your journey to adopt a posture of cultural humility. In sharing this, some of my clients and people in the audience say this resonates with them, as they have thought of it in the same way.

But not everyone immediately understands the subtle differences between these two concepts. If you are scratching your head and asking, "What's the difference?" keep reading! The following paragraphs explain the four attributes that help you develop a foundation of cultural competency, followed by a description of the key attributes that will help you adopt a posture of cultural humility.

It takes a lifetime commitment to constantly evaluate your awareness of how times are changing. This internal reflection leads to correcting the imbalance of power where we work and creating inclusive environments for all communities. Cultural competency is the foundation you will need to build on, so you can move toward developing a posture of cultural humility.

Four Attributes to Acquire a Foundation of Cultural Competency

Researchers Jesse Wilson, Colleen Ward, and Ronald Fischer defined cultural competency in 2013 as "the acquisition and maintenance of culture-specific skills."[21] In short, you need to be able to function effectively in new cultural contexts and interact effectively with people from different cultural backgrounds. Terry Cross and his associates in 1989 summarized cultural competency by saying that a person needs four attributes of self-awareness, attitude, knowledge, and cross-cultural skills to be culturally competent.[22]. A description of each of these attributes follows with questions for you to reflect on, so you can determine your level of competency in each of these areas.

Self-Awareness

How self-aware are you when it comes to your own culture? The awareness of your own culture is crucial to developing cultural competency and is foundational to developing a posture of cultural humility. I will talk more about this cornerstone of self-awareness in the following chapter.

Attitude

Do you acknowledge that it's OK for people to have different views than you? Your attitude should be one of a willingness to accept that others may have a different view and be OK with it.

Knowledge

Do you know much about different cultures? This requires reading, experiencing, traveling to different places, and talking with people from different cultures, so you can learn about their values and beliefs. You need to have a learning posture, knowing that culture influences a lot of how we do things—from business to the way we raise children.

Cross-Cultural Skills

Are you able to put into practice what you have learned about other cultures? This could be in how you communicate and interact with people from different cultures, not only verbally but nonverbally as well. Are you able to greet people from different cultural groups using what you learned about their greeting practices, such as hugging or bowing instead of shaking hands and not directly looking into the eyes of people from Asian countries? Communicating appropriately relies on cross-cultural skills. It is important to state that culture is the norm of a group and is *not* always related to ethnicity or race. This means that culture, at times, can be related to company culture, school culture, or geographic regions of the country. Many times, people only associate culture with ethnicity or race, but it is broader than that.

Three Attributes to Adopt a Posture of Cultural Humility

After you have gained the self-awareness, attitude, knowledge, and cross-cultural skills to reach cultural competency, you are ready to approach cultural humility. You may have read books, attended conferences and workshops, and even received a certificate in cultural competency. You are ready for the next step to be the exceptional leader you desire to be. What will it take for this to happen? Developing three key attributes will help you adopt a posture of cultural humility: a growth mindset, curiosity, and an ability to listen deeply.

Growth Mindset

Carol S. Dweck, a leading researcher in the fields of personality, social psychology, and developmental psychology, in her book, *Mindset: The New Psychology of Success,* identified that people have one of two mindsets when it comes to approaching success and setbacks: a fixed mindset or a growth mindset.[23]

Some people believe that no matter how hard they try to learn something they cannot, because they see it as a challenge that can't be overcome. Their mindset is fixed. For example, a leader says something he believes to be an innocent comment to a colleague from a minoritized group, but the comment offends his colleague. The leader is surprised by the offense. Although his colleague explains how his statement is offensive, it makes the leader feel small. He decides to play it safe and not say anything at all moving forward, because he believes that no matter how much he tries, he always says the wrong thing. So, this leader stops trying to engage in conversations about diversity, equity, inclusion, and belonging, becoming closed off to learning about his colleagues for fear of offending them. This is a missed opportunity to continue to learn and develop himself as an inclusive leader.

On the other hand, people with a growth mindset believe that even if they make mistakes, they can improve and take corrective action to be better communicators. In the example I just shared, the leader would take the colleague's feedback and see it as a learning opportunity, believing he could improve with a little work. He might possibly follow up with his colleague and ask to have a conversation if they are open to that, so he can learn from the experience. This approach will cultivate the leader's growth mindset.

There are other ways to cultivate a growth mindset. Seek out challenging tasks and projects that will stretch you personally or professionally. For me, that meant presenting at a conference, even though I had never facilitated a workshop or made a presentation outside of a classroom. What challenging task or project will stretch you?

We all make mistakes at work from time to time. Mistakes can be excellent opportunities to develop your growth mindset. The next time you realize you've made a mistake, reflect on what went wrong and what you can do differently moving forward, so it doesn't happen again. As you develop a growth mindset, you will move closer to developing cultural humility. But you will also need to develop curiosity. Let's talk about how you can do this.

Curiosity

As a White male leader, Tim was experiencing challenges with some of his team members of color who were frustrated that their organization was not making changes fast enough. They wanted to see more progress toward becoming a more inclusive organization that would inspire employees to develop a deep sense of belonging. He wasn't sure what more his organization could do to improve, as he believed leaders were doing everything possible.

After Tim described the challenge, I asked him if he could pose a question to his team members that would elicit some details to help him better understand their frustrations. He gave me a puzzled look. His first inclination was to be direct and just ask them what they wanted.

I asked, "How might they perceive your question?"

"Probably as confrontational."

"What open-ended question would allow your team members to reflect before responding?"

As we brainstormed how he could ask a question that would inspire reflection and positive, informative dialogue, I explained that open-ended questions can be powerful in helping people clarify their thoughts instead of asking close-ended questions. For example, asking someone "Why did you do that?" is a close-ended question. You could rephrase this as "What led you to make the decision you did?" When answering an open-ended question, people hear themselves respond, and it can evoke awareness and lead to change.

We agreed that he would ask his team members this question: "What does inclusion look like to you?" Tim realized this question would help him understand what inclusion meant for each of his team members. It would also help him think about how his organization needed to change, so it could develop the sense of belonging the organization's leaders had been talking about creating for their talent.

In our follow-up coaching session, Tim reported that he used this approach, and it led to a meaningful dialogue. He walked away knowing more fully what a sense of belonging looked like for his team members of color, specifically, how he could advocate for them more effectively.

Instead of confronting his team members to get the information he needed, Tim's approach required curiosity. Is it possible to develop your curiosity in social situations to better communicate with others? Yes, it is. Here are some exercises you can try, so you can further develop your curiosity.

- Ask why and what-if questions. For example: "Why do we always make decisions in our organization this way? What if we changed the way we make budgetary decisions?"

- Read books and articles, listen to podcasts, or watch documentaries that present different viewpoints than those you hold. From time to time, I watch a news channel that presents a different political view than mine, so I can hear the other side's perspective. I do this so I can hear things that challenge my viewpoint. This has helped me stay curious about my own ways of thinking.

- Visit unfamiliar places, including cities and
  museums, or attend cultural events. You could even
  attend presentations on topics you know nothing
  about, so you can experience new things to help
  generate a deeper interest in them.

As a coach I've been trained to be curious so I can help
my clients arrive at clarity about a challenge they may be
facing. This includes getting better at asking open-ended
questions that encourage my clients to be reflective. For
example, when someone says, "I can't do that," instead of
telling them what they need to do, perhaps start by exploring the things keeping them from accomplishing the task
they've set out to do. Ask what it would take to eliminate the
barriers keeping them from accomplishing their goal.

This type of questioning gives a person the agency to
identify what they need to do to accomplish their task.
The next time you find yourself wanting to ask a direct or
close-ended question, stop and think about how you can
rephrase that question so it is open-ended and creates space
for reflection.

Here are three more examples to help you think about
how you can use open-ended questions to develop your
curiosity. In the first example, perhaps you supervise someone who is not sure how to approach a challenge and is
coming to you for direction and just wants you to tell them
what to do. You can ask them, "What's worked in the past?"
This open-ended question may help them unlock a mem-
ory that can guide them in their current scenario. This is
an excellent opportunity to develop your curiosity! You can
ask several follow-up questions to help them recall details

of that past project, which they may be able to apply to their current project.

Another example is when one of your team members presents a challenge that you know has an underlying issue. Instead of just telling them what you believe to be the issue, a way to practice and show curiosity is to ask them, "What do you believe the real issue is?" This will provide the team member an opportunity to learn to be reflective instead of relying on you for the answer. A question like this gets them to dig deeper. You can follow up with additional open-ended questions so you can help them identify the underlying issue and move toward a solution. Simultaneously, this practice helps you develop your curiosity.

The last example has to do with how to use curiosity to lead meetings. Instead of starting by telling people what the agenda/topic will be, lead with the following question: "What would make our meeting today a success for you?" A question like this makes the other people feel like they are valued and that you are there to support them. Of course, it's important to truly be curious in this situation. Listen closely to each person's comment and ask follow-up questions for clarification. Then adjust the agenda or topic, as appropriate, to reflect their input. These examples illustrate how you can use curiosity to lead more exceptionally.

As I have developed my curiosity, I've come to realize this is an important component of having a posture of cultural humility. To develop your curiosity, you must develop the ability to listen deeply so you can ask questions that evoke awareness. Let's talk about what deep listening can look like.

Listening Deeply

In his book, *How to Listen: Discover the Hidden Key to Better Communication,* Oscar Trimboli describes the importance of preparing to listen. He compares it to the way orchestras prepare to perform by tuning their instruments.[24] You must learn how to "tune" your brain so you can listen to and hear what the other person is saying. This is key in developing the ability to remain curious, especially when engaging in conversations related to diversity, equity, inclusion, and belonging.

Offenses often occur when we work toward creating more inclusive organizations because we don't take time to listen. Generally, we try to convince the other person that we are right instead of taking time to listen to what the person is saying. This means we miss the underlying issue and jump to conclusions. We're seeking to convince instead of seeking to understand.

So, how do you learn to "tune" your brain to listen more deeply? Oscar Trimboli states that it begins by learning how to listen to yourself through a breathing exercise. First, notice how you are breathing, fixing your eyes on a blank wall and away from screens and turning off your electronic devices. When you do this for three minutes, you will notice the thoughts that are distracting you and become more aware of your wandering thoughts.[25] This will help you prepare to focus on your upcoming conversation.

Box breathing is another breathing exercise that can help you hone your listening skills. Inhale for four seconds, hold your breath for four seconds, breathe out for four seconds, and hold for four seconds. It is called a box because you mentally begin drawing a box with a four-second inhale (vertical line), then hold your breath for four seconds (horizontal line), then a four-second exhale (vertical line), and then hold for four seconds (horizontal line that closes the box). See Figure 2.

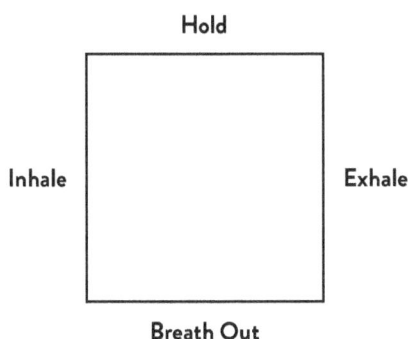

Hold

```
Inhale  ┌─────────┐  Exhale
        │         │
        │         │
        │         │
        └─────────┘
```

Breath Out

Figure 2. Box Breathing

This exercise helps you listen to your breathing, so the next time you are in a conversation, you can become more aware of what your body is doing and what might be distracting you from listening attentively.

Turning off your electronic devices before starting a conversation is another effective strategy to help with your listening skills. You can also try putting your phone on Do Not Disturb. In his research, Trimboli states that 86 percent of the respondents in his study reported that turning off their devices made the most improvement on their ability to listen.[26]

The goal is to become conscious of your thoughts, not to eliminate them. Setting aside the thoughts that distract you from listening attentively will keep your conversations from becoming disjointed. The idea is learning to listen to yourself first before entering into a conversation, so you can be fully present, listen deeply, and remain curious. Otherwise, you could miss important points people are saying, keeping you from developing a posture of cultural humility.

I would like to share an example. I was about to enter a coaching session with a client, and just ahead of the session I was consumed with thinking about how to make sure I had enough time later that night to pick up one of our kids from school and then make it back home in time to make dinner for the family. Doing a breathing exercise helped clear my mind and prepare me to listen to my client more deeply and with curiosity.

Listening is a key component to moving from cultural competency to cultural humility and to start being an inclusive leader, which can seem like an elusive role, but it is possible. It is important to start with cultural competency, but as I have shared, it doesn't stop there if you want to reach cultural humility.

If you believe you need to develop a growth mindset, curiosity, or the ability to listen better, take time to start doing so. Practicing the exercises in this chapter will help you get started. Ask a mentor or professional coach to help you process the exercises and create a space to be reflective, so you can note what you are learning and identify the areas that need improvement.

The journey toward cultural humility isn't only for the workplace, and in my own life I have come to realize that cultural competency is only part of the puzzle. Let me share a personal example of what cultural humility looks like for me outside of my organizational context.

It was like any other weekday. Seth, one of our four kids, had left the house and was walking to middle school. My wife had just left for work, and I was drinking my morning coffee. A text came in from Seth.

My jaw dropped as I read the message.

"Sorry I'm texting this to you, but I don't know how to say it out loud. I want to ask you two things. The first is that you start referring to me by my preferred name, Jayden. I prefer it, because it is gender fluid. The second thing I'd like to ask you is for financial aid in buying a more feminine wardrobe to better keep in touch with my gender fluidity."

Their message left me dazed and confused and with lots of questions. All the cultural competency workshops I had attended did not prepare me for this. I thought I knew about gender and sexual identity, but I did not. This is a real-life example of how having a posture of curiosity, listening, and a growth mindset can help you navigate a complex situation. I was able to think about how to create a space for Jayden as they (pronouns are they/them) explore their gender identity, and I could explore my role as a father raising a gender-fluid child.

My spouse and I had fostered safety for Jayden over many years. Their coming out to us affirmed that they trusted us, even if the method they used was via text: this method of communication felt most comfortable to them. My spouse and I were pleased that they felt safe enough to tell us about their newly discovered identity.

I knew the specific approaches that worked as a culturally competent leader would not work in this situation, because much of what I had learned only centered on race and ethnicity, not on gender identity. However, the posture of cultural humility I had adopted did work, since this allowed me to remain curious when I didn't fully understand Jayden's journey.

Jayden's identity will continue to evolve, and this requires me to be comfortable with ambiguity, even when it feels uncomfortable. This experience crystallized for me why stopping at cultural competency is not enough if you want to lead exceptionally in your home or your organization and why it's important to move forward to the next step: cultural humility. Having a posture of cultural humility can help you learn to be comfortable with the continued evolution of people's identities and help you lead diversity, equity, inclusion, and belonging efforts exceptionally.

You may be wondering if I received permission to share this story. Rest assured that I asked Jayden to read this section of the book before including this story, and they gave me permission to share it.

When you have cultural self-awareness, a positive attitude, knowledge of other cultures, and the skills to effectively work with people from other cultures, you have a clear picture of cultural competency and what is necessary to begin to develop cultural humility. I would like to remind you that cultural humility involves internal, personal work; the external work of correcting power imbalances in organizations; and creating systems that promote inclusive communities. I will describe each of these characteristics and how to develop them in Chapters 4 through 6. I invite you to read on using a growth mindset instead of a fixed mindset as you develop a posture of cultural humility.

Take Action

> In this chapter I shared several exercises to help you develop a growth mindset, curiosity, and the ability to listen more deeply. Take time to review the exercises and commit to trying each one during the next two weeks. Write down your reflections on what you learned about yourself and share those reflections with a trusted colleague, mentor, or your professional coach.

> Take the Cultural Humility Assessment on my website, www.DearWhiteLeader.com, to determine where you are on my cultural humility scale and share the results with someone you trust to get feedback.

CHAPTER 4

Self-Awareness and
Self-Critique

I YAWNED AND SAT BACK in my chair, glancing at the clock on my computer screen. In a little less than an hour I was going to head home to be with my family after a long day at work. I heard a knock on my office door and said, "Come in." It was Katherine, one of my direct reports. She asked if I had a minute. I said, "Yes, I do." I was not sure what this was about, but I was always available to my team.

Katherine asked, "Is it OK if I give you some feedback about this morning's team meeting?" I said of course. She then shared the following: "Are you aware that you tend to listen to the people in the meeting who are the most vocal and that are men?" I was stunned to hear this, as I always thought I was inclusive in how I led.

I responded by saying, "I had no idea."

She then said this had been something she had been wanting to share with me for some time, but finally felt she could. I immediately apologized for what I had been doing and thanked her for bringing it to my attention. She provided me with specific examples, and I made sure to listen attentively. She finished and left my office.

This was a watershed moment for me. Having been involved in diversity, equity, inclusion, and belonging efforts for many years I believed, like many who do this work, that these things shouldn't happen to me. I should be better! This experience crystallized the fact that being an inclusive leader requires a commitment to lifelong learning and can be elusive.

Another point to remember is that no matter how much you learn you will have to give yourself grace, as you will make mistakes along the way. This is important to remember, so you don't beat yourself up to the point that you give up on your efforts to develop a posture of cultural humility. As I shared in Chapter 3, you will want to have a growth mindset so you can learn from your mistakes and pick yourself up off the floor and keep moving forward.

Developing a posture of cultural humility requires acknowledging that you have biases, that they will continue to be prevalent, and that working to mitigate their impact is imperative if you are going to develop cultural humility. It also requires acknowledging that the work of getting better at diversity, equity, inclusion, and belonging for yourself and your organization is not a specific destination or something to be achieved, like a task you cross off your to-do list. It requires a posture of cultural humility, so you can be comfortable with being uncomfortable and a willingness to continue to develop so your organization can truly be inclusive.

As I have shared, it is important to develop three components of cultural humility. The first characteristic is self-awareness and self-critique. This is the internal work you must do. As you saw in Figure 1, the other two components are changing systems in your organization (the systemic work) and redressing power imbalances (the external work).

Knowing the biases you have, and how to mitigate their impact, will be helpful in developing a posture of cultural humility.

Becoming Aware of Our Innate Biases

What is bias? The *Cambridge Dictionary* defines bias as "the action of supporting or opposing a particular person in an unfair way, because of allowing personal opinions to influence your judgment."[27] *Psychology Today* describes bias as something that is innate in us that forms negative ideas about people, individuals, or ideas that we learn and relies on areas such as socioeconomic status, race, ethnicity, national origin, and so forth.

Bias can adversely impact the way we view people in both our personal and professional lives.[28] For example, when I was a kid in the 1980s, I watched a lot of news about crime that was happening in my city, Los Angeles. The news I was seeing created a negative stereotype for me that people who perpetrated crime were poor and people of color, which is not the case. Yet because of my propensity to form negative ideas about people, I allowed the media to create and reinforce the stereotype. As I have matured and seen the data about crime, I learned that this stereotype was incorrect.

This has played out in my career by ensuring I create space and check myself before meetings. I do this by asking myself, "What bias do I need to check myself about before this meeting starts?" This exercise has helped me mitigate the impact that bias has in how I lead and interact with people.

Several types of biases exist, and you might want to look at all of them as this might be something to explore for yourself. For the purposes of this book, I will discuss three types of biases that directly impede our ability to develop cultural humility: unconscious or implicit bias, confirmation bias, and affinity bias.

Unconscious or Implicit Bias

The *Cambridge Dictionary* explains that the person with the unconscious bias is not aware of it, and it can influence decisions in recruitment, promotion, and performance management.[29] The story I shared at the opening of this chapter is an example of one of the unconscious biases that I hold. These biases tend to play out the most when it comes to trying to develop a more inclusive organization with a strong sense of belonging and can hinder your progress toward developing a posture of cultural humility. It is important that you begin to uncover what those might be, so you can develop a plan to mitigate their impact.

In their book *Blindspot: Hidden Biases of Good People,*[30] psychologists Mahzarin R. Banaji and Anthony G. Greenwald present years of research with over one million people related to biases about age, gender, race, ethnicity, religion, social class, and so forth. They share how these biases show up at work and in personal lives and the negative impact they can have on people. For example, according to their research, most White Americans associate good things with White people rather than good things with Black people.

Another example they share has to do with gender bias. For example, a doctor may decide not to conduct a cholesterol lab test on a woman because of their belief that women have a lower risk of heart disease. This stereotype can have a negative impact on the women they are treating and could have lifelong consequences.

This may be hard for you to read, and you might deny that this is a reality or that this is your reality. The point is, we all have biases related to a lot of things that live in our unconscious thoughts. The biases we hold impact every facet of our lives and show up in ways that can negatively impact the way we lead and keep us from leading exceptionally.

In reading their book I was made aware of a tool that can help us discover the types of biases we hold. That assessment is the Implicit Bias Association Test (IAT). The IAT is an assessment offered at no cost and offers ninety different topics that a person can use to assess both their conscious and unconscious preferences.

After reading the book I took an assessment. In discovering the biases I held, I was able to develop a plan to mitigate their impact on the way I lead. The first step is discovering and acknowledging that I had biases. The IAT was instrumental in helping me do this. I then shared the results with people who knew me well and asked them if they had observed the biases in some fashion. This usually led to a discussion about specific examples they had observed about my biases. After listening well (this meant not being defensive), I then developed a strategy to mitigate their impact and a process to remind myself that I had these biases. In the case of the feedback from my direct report, Katherine, this meant that before every meeting I would take time to remind myself about the bias. This helped to ensure I did not repeat the mistakes that Katherine had pointed out to me. This has helped me mitigate the impact of my biases.

I use this same approach when working with my cultural humility coaching clients, and it has served them well. In working with my White cultural humility coaching client, Felicia, we agreed that taking the IAT would help her identify the biases that she held. After taking the IAT she was able to recognize that, although identifying as a woman, she had a bias toward men. We then spent time discussing how this bias has shown up for her in her role as an executive. She shared that it tends to show up in the meetings she runs so, like myself, she agreed that before meetings she would spend time reminding herself about the bias to minimize the likelihood of the bias presenting itself in meetings. She reported that this had been helpful for her.

I encourage you to take the IAT online assessment, so you can begin to uncover the biases that will keep you from developing cultural humility. After taking the assessment, spend time reflecting on how the biases you have present themselves in your daily work life. That could mean making hiring decisions, running a meeting, or interacting with an employee or colleague.

Confirmation Bias

The second type of bias that can rear its ugly head when it comes to developing cultural humility is confirmation bias. The *Cambridge Dictionary* defines confirmation bias as "the fact that people are more likely to accept or notice information if it appears to support what they already believe or expect."[31] This has shown up in my own life in how I view the topic of immigration. I am the son of immigrants, and this fact greatly influences my point of view on this topic. I don't like hearing from people who have an opposing view, so I have tended to surround myself with people who hold my view. Recently I have been stretching myself to hear from people who hold a different view.

This type of bias can also be detrimental to developing a posture of cultural humility. It can impact your ability to listen for differences in how people might think about diversity, equity, inclusion, and belonging. We tend to want to surround ourselves with people who agree with us. Sometimes this is a good thing, like when you need encouragement and friendship with people who think like you to sustain you. This is necessary, at times, but if you want to develop cultural humility you will want to spend time with people who think differently than you, so you can hear different perspectives. If you don't, you will allow confirmation bias to keep you from learning about things that are necessary for you and your organization to be more inclusive and to develop that sense of belonging you want to create.

Another way to remember the dangers of confirmation bias is to remember the leadership wisdom that many leaders are taught early in their careers but struggle to apply. You want people in your organization who think differently than you do so you can avoid groupthink, which can keep organizations from developing tunnel vision. This means making a conscious effort to not let this happen, because your tendency may be to surround yourself with people who think like you. Just as being an exceptional leader requires you to avoid group thinking, the same goes for developing a posture of cultural humility. You need to be able to be with people who think differently and remain curious in those moments.

Affinity Bias

The last type of bias that I would like to point out is affinity bias. This type of bias is when we favor people who share a characteristic, such as graduating from the same college or attending the same church. This bias can become problematic when we favor people in our affinity groups over others, particularly when it comes to hiring or promoting people in organizations because they belong to groups that we have an affinity toward.

How has this shown up for me? When I was in a C-suite executive position I tended to favor applicants who had the same types of degrees I had, thinking this would help them be better in their roles. In my professional life I have had to remind myself that this has not always been my experience. This may seem trivial, but it can be problematic and can lead to keeping us from developing a posture of cultural humility by contributing to confirmation bias.

I encourage you to complete the Circle of Trust exercise[32] to help you identify the people you may tend to favor in your sphere of influence. Using Figure 3, identify five to ten people in the first column whom you consider to be in your circle of trust. Then add categories (anywhere from five to nine columns) that can include race/ethnicity, gender, sexual orientation, age, education level, and so forth. You then place an X in the columns for the people who share the same categories as you.

When you are done you may notice that most, if not all, the people in your circle of trust are the same gender as you or share the same race/ethnicity. This may reveal that you favor people who share your gender or sexual identity. The point is that you may notice a pattern that is keeping you from having people with different identities than your own in your circle. This exercise may reveal that you have affinity biases, and you may want to take the necessary steps to address them so you can move toward developing a posture of cultural humility. Once you identify the type of affinity biases you hold, you can then develop a plan to put yourself in spaces with people outside of the groups you tend to gravitate to so you can expand your network.

Now that you know about these three types of biases and have a tool you can use to identify your implicit biases, I would like to introduce you to what it looks like to develop cultural self-awareness.

Category	Race/ Ethnicity	Gender	Sexual Orientation	Age	Education Level	?	?	?
Person 1								
Person 2								
Person 3								
Person 4								
Person 5								

Figure 3. The Circle of Trust Exercise

Cultural Self-Awareness

Cultural self-awareness is the process of identifying how culture has influenced you and how you navigate cultural differences in your life. Knowing this will help you immensely in developing a posture of cultural humility.

How does someone become culturally self-aware? An instrument that can help you identify how you navigate cultural differences is the Intercultural Development Inventory (IDI). This instrument will tell you where you are along the Intercultural Development Continuum (IDC).[33] The IDC describes a person's or a group's orientation toward cultural differences.

The IDI indicates what a person sees or does not see related to cultural differences inside and outside the workplace. It consists of five developmental orientations: denial, polarization, minimization, acceptance, and adaptation. After taking the assessment, you're placed in one of the five orientations. It's important to note that the continuum is fluid, and a person can move along the continuum in either direction, depending on life circumstances that can impact how one views themselves and others related to cultural differences. It is also developmental, meaning that if a person puts in the effort, they can move from one orientation to another.

Let's look at the five developmental orientations:

- **Denial** reflects limited experience and capability for understanding and responding to cultural differences having to do with values, beliefs, perceptions, emotional responses, and behaviors.

- **Polarization** refers to a mindset that views cultural differences from an "us versus them" perspective, meaning that someone may value another person's culture with higher regard than their own. It could also mean that someone views their own culture with higher regard than someone else's.

- **Minimization** references the stage in which people tend to focus on cultural similarities when they experience cultural differences because they may not want to experience conflict. It may also mean that they have a limited understanding of their own cultural identity.

- **Acceptance** is the stage in which people see and appreciate cultural differences. They also have a curiosity about other cultures and want to learn more about them.

- **Adaptation** is the stage in which people can navigate appropriately between cultural groups. They are able to shift their behavior in culturally appropriate ways. They are also able to recognize cultural differences and are comfortable with conflict that may arise from those differences.

The IDI measures where people are along the continuum and which stage they may be in. It also assesses where you perceive yourself to be and where you actually are along the continuum. When I first took the assessment, I landed in minimization. As a person of color who at the time was heavily involved in leading diversity, equity, inclusion, and belonging efforts, I believed I would have been further along on the continuum. When I met with a Qualified Administrator of the IDI to discuss the results, I shared my frustration. She pointed out that one of the characteristics of people in minimization, particularly those from a minoritized community, is that we may minimize our own cultural identities in order to find success in our professional contexts. It's the idea of "going along to get along." This resonated with me, as I wanted to get things done when it came to my organization making the changes necessary to become more inclusive and wanted the changes to happen with the least amount of conflict.

Moving along the continuum is a developmental process. Just because you are in the minimization stage when you first take the assessment does not mean that you cannot move along the continuum after putting in the effort to develop your cultural competency.

I am now a Qualified Administrator, and I use this tool extensively in coaching individuals toward developing a posture of cultural humility, as one of the necessary steps is becoming more culturally self-aware and becoming more effective at bridging cultural differences.

I encourage you to find a Qualified Administrator who can administer the assessment so you can identify where you are along the continuum and then create a strategy to develop your ability to bridge cultural differences. A benefit of taking the assessment and meeting with a Qualified Administrator is that you will also receive an intercultural development plan along with your profile. This tool will help you move along the continuum and build your capacity to bridge cultural differences.

I have worked with clients who have started at minimization and ended at adaptation. They were able to move along the continuum by doing the work needed to do so. This involved working through the exercises in their intercultural development plan. As with any assessment it's important that you don't just take it, but that you use it to develop yourself. If you're going to be an exceptional leader it will not be enough to just know where you are on the continuum, but you must make the effort to move along the continuum.

Another key piece that I believe is necessary in developing your cultural humility is identifying which social identities are salient for you and how they show up in your personal and professional life. This is a key aspect of developing cultural self-awareness.

How Many Social Identities Do You Have?

You may not realize it, but you have multiple social identities. These are your identities that you identify based on group memberships. They could be your race, ethnicity, gender, sexual identity, faith, ability, national origin, and so forth. This is an important aspect of self-awareness because it will help you determine how people may be relating to you and how your identities impact the way you navigate cultural differences.

An exercise that can help you identify which of your social identities are salient for you is called the Social Identity Wheel.[34] This exercise will help you identify and reflect on how your identities become visible and may be felt as you interact with people around you.

In this exercise, four questions are the most important:

1. Which identities do you think of most often?
2. Which identities do you think of least often?
3. Which identities do you want to learn more about?
4. Which identities have the strongest effect on how you perceive yourself?

When I facilitate this exercise with clients it leads to having a deep discussion about how they perceive themselves and how others might perceive them. For example, if one of your salient identities is your sexual identity, I would ask, "How does your sexual identity show up for you in the way you lead or are perceived?" A client may say, "It does not show up, because I do not feel comfortable sharing that identity with people." I would then follow up with a question like, "Do you like the way that feels?" Most of my clients have answered no to this question. We then talk about what it would look like to become comfortable sharing their sexual identity. The importance of leading authentically means being comfortable with who you are and eliminating the idea of having to hide who you are.

We then talk about how they can remove the barriers for the people they lead who may believe they have to hide who they are when they are at work. Doing this exercise can go a long way in creating psychological safety for your team, which I detailed in Chapter 2.

The other meaningful conversation is around the question of which identities you want to learn more about. This usually is related to learning about your cultural roots.

I have worked with clients who, after doing this exercise, discover that they want to learn more about their ethnicity. They realize this can help them bridge cultural differences more effectively, as it's an important component to becoming more culturally self-aware.

This may mean learning more about identity development. In working with my clients to help them get clear on their identities, this sometimes leads them to realize that some of their identities give them privileges they were not aware of, particularly privileges related to social identities. For example, you may have a visceral reaction to the term *White privilege*, as it gets a lot of negative attention. However, understanding that you have privilege is an important aspect of self-awareness and self-critique and will help you develop a posture of cultural humility.

It is important to understand that there are two categories when it comes to privilege. They are earned and unearned privilege, and there is a difference.

Earned versus Unearned Privilege

Even as a person of color, I have come to realize that I have privileges that have afforded me opportunities that others do not have. As a cisgender, heterosexual male, United States citizen, and a person of color who can pass as White, I have had access to opportunities that some do not have. For example, as a cisgender heterosexual male, I do not have to worry about the possibility of experiencing violence because of my sexual and gender identity. I do not have to always think about whether I am being paid what I am worth like those who identify as women. As a

United States citizen, I can vote and had access to resources like federal financial aid, which people who are undocumented cannot get even though they have been educated in our public school system from kindergarten to the twelfth grade. People assume that I am a White person, and this has given me the ability to feel confident when applying for jobs because I do not have to worry about being discriminated against for the color of my skin.

The unearned privilege I have been afforded has made it easier for me to achieve earned privileges. I have a doctorate degree and am part of the upper middle class. This gives me privileges like being automatically given creditability because of the degrees I've earned and the professional positions I've held. This gives me the ability to purchase items for myself and my family that, early in my life, I could not dream of owning, because my parents were living paycheck to paycheck. This realization has been eye-opening for me and has caused me to reflect on the privileges I have and how I can use them to redress the power imbalances I have seen as an organization leader.

Acknowledging that you have privilege as a White person is an important step in self-awareness and self-critique. Why is this important? It is important because acknowledging it will allow you to be in spaces with people from marginalized communities, and you can empathize with them and advocate for them. You have privileges that you have earned by overcoming challenges just as those whom you lead or are in your social sphere.

You can begin to reflect on your privileges by first thinking about which privileges you have, both earned and unearned, and writing them down. Once you have done this, think about how they manifest themselves in your personal and professional life. I suggest you discuss these thoughts with others, and when someone points out your privileges stay curious in that moment and do not get defensive. This will help you begin to acknowledge your privileges with others. Finally, once you recognize your privileges, consider how you can use them to advocate for others and redress the power imbalances you notice in your organization. This exercise will go a long way to help you develop a posture of cultural humility.

To develop a posture of cultural humility it is not enough for you to work on self-awareness; you will also need to work on other awareness. What might that look like?

Other Awareness

As I shared in Chapter 3, you will need to develop the ability to be curious. Your ability to be curious will help you gain a deeper awareness of others and their identities. This is an important aspect of cultural humility so you can gain an appreciation for who they are and their salient identities. As was the case for you to know your social identities, it will be helpful for you to know about their identities and how they show up with them within your organization. This will help you as a leader recognize the challenges those from marginalized communities have faced in their lives and possibly the challenges they have faced in your organization.

In Chapter 5 I will discuss the importance of addressing the power imbalances that exist in your organization. For you to recognize those imbalances it will be important to gain awareness of others in the organization you serve, lead, or have influence in.

A way to develop other awareness is to consider the cultural iceberg theory[35] developed by Edward Hall in 1976, a White male interculturalist. The cultural iceberg theory can be described this way: You generally only see 10 to 15 percent of an iceberg above sea level, but if you were to look under the surface of the sea you will see an expansive body of ice. Like an iceberg, there is more to us than just what people see. If you were to spend time getting to know someone you would find out more about them than how they present.

For instance, I present as White, but if you were to talk with me you would find out that I identify as Mexican American. In addition, you would also find out that I am a father and have a family, and that my faith is very important to me. You would not have known that until talking with me.

To gain a deeper awareness of others you have to get to know them. You have to develop your curiosity about people. Culture is more than just race and ethnicity; it encompasses faith, beliefs, values, gender, socioeconomic status, and sexual identity and orientation. Take time to think about the people around you. How much do you know about the cultural identities they hold? Are you only relying on what you see, or are you taking an interest in getting to know them or what is below "sea level"?

Try an exercise from Jennifer Brown's book, *How to Be an Inclusive Leader: Your Role in Creating Cultures of Belonging Where Everyone Can Thrive*.[36] Draw an iceberg on a sheet of paper and label the identities you hold that people can see about you and then list the identities that lie below sea level. See Figure 4 as an example.

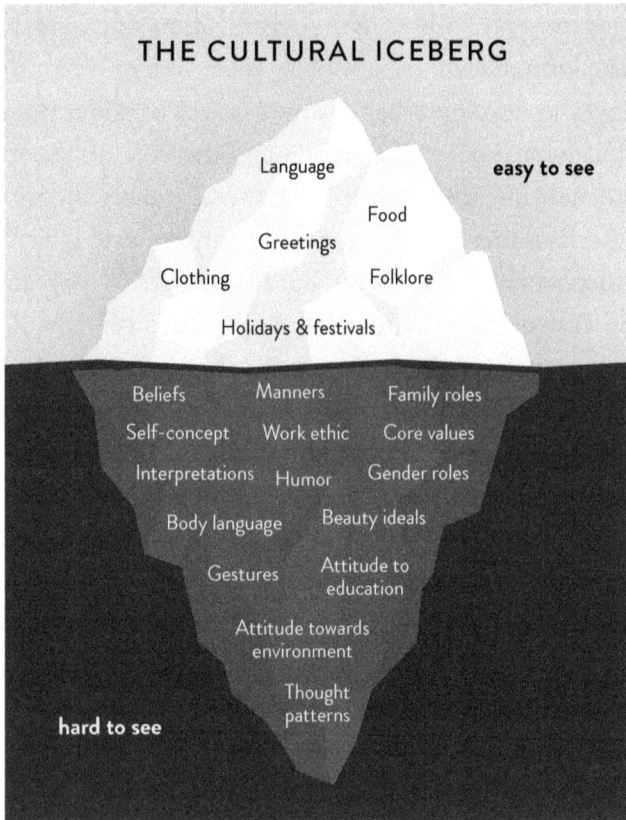

Figure 4. Cultural Iceberg

After completing this exercise, ask yourself these three questions:

1. What identities do you allow others to see?
2. What identities do you keep hidden below sea level?
3. What would make you let others see below sea level?

Now that you have answered these questions for yourself, take time to think about the people around you and how they might answer these same three questions. This reflective exercise will help you develop a deeper level of awareness around your identities, and it will help you reflect on people around you and why they share (or are not able to share) their identities with you or others in your organization. You may realize that the culture in the organization does not provide the psychological safety needed so people in your organization can bring their full selves to work.

What is the outcome? When people do not feel psychologically safe to bring their full selves to work, they leave the organization because they do not feel valued and appreciated. The cost to an organization that cannot keep its talent is extremely high and is an expensive proposition. According to Gallup, the cost of replacing a salaried employee can range from one-half to two times the employee's annual salary.[37] Creating psychological safety will go a long way in helping you keep your talent and helping your organization develop a sense of belonging.

Mary, a White female client, expressed a strong desire to get to know the people she leads at a deeper level or know what is "below sea level" for her team. She asked me what she can do to "lower the sea level" for people. I asked, "What are some things that people you reported to do to make you feel comfortable sharing about yourself?" She replied that they shared about themselves first. I then asked, "What is keeping you from sharing about yourself?" The lightbulb went off for Mary. She realized the importance of modeling the behavior she would like to see in her team members.

We agreed that the best way to do this is when she has individual meetings with her team members. She would share more about herself, specifically about her experience as a woman in her organization. As we worked together, she shared that by doing this she had been able to create a level of comfort with her team members that led them to share more about their identities with her.

Like Mary, you can lead your team members to have inclusion safety, one of the four quadrants of psychological safety discussed in Chapter 2. (Recall that the four quadrants of psychological safety are learner, challenger, collaborator, and inclusion safety.) Inclusion safety has to do with team members knowing they are valued, safe to treat all people fairly, and feel that their experiences and ideas matter.

Developing other awareness will go a long way in helping you develop a posture of cultural humility. Developing a posture of cultural humility is complex and will require retraining yourself, but it can be done. It will require risk-taking and being comfortable with being uncomfortable. This can be difficult for leaders to grasp, because we always want to be in control, and we always want to make the complex simple to set ourselves up for success. Unfortunately, navigating diversity, equity, inclusion, and belonging is complex and requires a level of comfort that sometimes can be difficult to arrive at. What are some things you can do to help you navigate the complexity?

Navigating the Complexity of DEIB

The pandemic, if anything, made us realize that our world is complex and will continue to be that way for the foreseeable future. No longer will we have predictability in our personal and professional lives. The worldwide demonstrations in support of racial justice that took place after the murder of George Floyd in 2020 and the ongoing violence against members of the Asian American Pacific Islander and LGBTQ+ communities have made visible the inequities that exist in our country. These experiences have become part of our workplaces and have added to the complexity we find ourselves in today. As leaders we desire predictability, which makes it more challenging, as we tend to want easy answers to complex situations. The reality is that if you are going to be a leader in this area, you have to become comfortable with complexity.

In their book *Unleash Your Complexity Genius: Growing Your Inner Capacity to Lead,* leadership experts Jennifer Garvey Berger and Carolyn Coughlin share how leaders need to become aware of what complexity does to us physically and how to retrain our nervous system to develop the skills necessary to navigate the complexity we are experiencing and will be experiencing in the years to come.

So, how do you become comfortable with uncertainty and manage your nervous system? Berger and Coughlin share eight practices you can do to develop your comfort and the ability to unleash your "complexity genius." These eight practices are: noticing, breathing, moving, sleeping, laughing, wondering, experimenting, and loving.[38]

Noticing

According to the authors, in this stage it is important to notice what is happening around you before giving into the urge to act. For example, at work you are experiencing a tense situation between you and your supervisor that may lead you to go directly to your supervisor to confront them, which can go wrongly for you if you do it without developing an approach that invites dialogue. If you have developed the ability to notice before acting, you may recognize the source of the tension that has been created. You can easily do this by pausing, closing your eyes, and breathing. Doing these things will create space for you to reflect on your situation, leading to the recognition of the source of the problem before doing something you may regret.

Breathing

Learning how to use breathing techniques will help you focus and listen, as I shared in Chapter 3. Breathing will help you be a better listener so you can hear people more deeply, leading to having a better understanding of where that person is coming from. You will have a better idea of what you need to do to lead exceptionally in the areas of diversity, equity, inclusion, and belonging. Learning how to use breathing techniques is important, as it will help you slow down and will help you tap into the creativity you will need to address the complex challenges you are experiencing.

Moving

If you are going to unleash your complexity genius, you need to cultivate a discipline of exercise. You need to get moving by exercising. Try running or dancing to the point where you run out of breath. Moving could include going for walks, working in your backyard, or stretching on a consistent basis. This will unleash the creativity in your nervous system.

Sleeping

You need to treat sleep as a leadership habit or discipline. This means making it a priority so you are well rested. This could also mean placing your smartphone away from your bedside table, so you are not tempted to reach for it if you wake up in the middle of the night. The three practices I just described—noticing, breathing, and moving—are physical and necessary to ground you in your own body, which directly impacts your healthy sleep habits. We must learn to trust our own bodies and what they are telling us about what is happening around us, which goes a long way in retraining our nervous system.

Experimenting

This means you need to let go of your desire to fix things. You need to hold things loosely. This does not mean letting go of things completely; it's more like when you hold sand in your hands and allow it to slowly fall through the cracks of your hands. If you learn how to do this, you will experience less frustration when experiencing a complex situation, and you will be OK with trying different approaches and remaining curious in moments when you are seeking to understand. By practicing this attitude of experimenting, you will begin to press into the cultural humility you are developing and allow yourself to listen to voices of people around you whom you may have not listened to before.

Laughing

Learning how to laugh in a variety of situations (even in those stressful moments), will also help you learn to be comfortable with complexity and navigate complexity. Seeing and laughing at the irony in the complexity in things is important to managing your nervous system. Of course, you need to be careful how you use laughter in the moment, as it may not be received well. The point is that you need to be mindful of the context.

Wondering

What I mean by this is looking at things with a sense of amazement. This will become more natural as you develop your curiosity. A way to do this is to think about times in your life when you experienced something that amazed you. Perhaps you are experiencing a challenging situation related to diversity, equity, inclusion, and belonging. Asking these questions welcomes wonderment: What is it about the situation you find yourself in that is causing you anxiety? What has you stuck? Reflecting on these questions will allow your sense of wonderment to kick in and may help you navigate the complex scenario you find yourself in.

Loving

A way to practice loving that will help you manage your nervous system during complexity is noticing the differences that exist around you, particularly in the people you lead, and gaining a loving appreciation for them. It could also mean writing down things that you are grateful for related to leading exceptionally in the work of diversity, equity, inclusion, and belonging.

Another way you can think about becoming comfortable with complexity and uncertainty is what neuroscientist, psychologist, and author Lisa Feldman Barrett has uncovered. She states that "uncertainty is more unpleasant and arousing than assured harm, because if the future is a mystery, you can't prepare for it." She also shares that "when people are seriously ill but have an excellent chance of recovery, they are less satisfied with life than people who know their disease is permanent."[39] Reflect on that for a minute or two! This translates to being OK with certainty, even if the outcome is dying, compared to how something might possibly end. Our brains want certainty! Yet, as I have shared, being an exceptional leader in this area means you must be OK with uncertainty.

Learning to be comfortable with complexity will help you tremendously when it comes to developing cultural humility. It will take time. All the ideas I have shared about developing self-awareness and self-critique will help you begin to move from cultural competency to cultural humility. An important point to keep in mind is that you cannot do this alone. You will need people around you to help you develop self-awareness and self-critique. To make this point I would like to share a metaphor that I believe highlights the importance of working with people to further your personal growth.

California's redwood trees grow to be immensely tall and, like other trees, grow alongside the same type of trees. Most people think they have deep roots, but they do not. They have a shallow root system. What makes them strong and able to withstand fierce winds and storms is that their roots are intertwined. In other words, their roots grow outward and lock together with the roots of the other trees growing alongside them.

The work of developing self-awareness and self-critique requires people to help you, and this cannot be done in isolation. Like the redwood tree, you need to work with your community to develop your self-awareness and self-critique. I have provided you with the tools to work toward developing a posture of cultural humility, but these tools will only get you so far. You need to work with others to navigate the complexities you will experience as you develop yourself to be an exceptional leader.

Your community might consist of your colleagues, family, faith community, or others you trust, such as a professional coach. Having a coach and mentor you can partner with will provide the level of accountability you will need to develop self-awareness and provide you with the feedback that can facilitate the self-critique you will need as you move from cultural competency toward cultural humility. The process starts with self-awareness and self-critique; this is the foundation of developing a posture of cultural humility, and you cannot skip it.

In the opening story, I shared how I was impacted by Katherine coming to me to share what she was observing in my leadership. This created a moment of self-awareness that prompted me to recognize what I needed to do to become a more inclusive leader. If I had not listened to her feedback and taken a posture of curiosity, I would not have been able to become a better leader. You can do the same.

Now that you know what self-awareness and self-critique look like and how to develop them, you will learn how to identify and redress the power imbalances that may exist in your organization.

Take Action

I have given you a lot to think about and do in this chapter. You may want to give yourself a period of three months to work through these exercises, so you can give them the attention they need. I encourage you to ask others to keep you accountable by doing these exercises with them, taking the metaphor of the redwood trees and bringing it to life.

➤ Take the Implicit Association Test (IAT) and share the results with people you trust. Ask for their feedback about the results and if they have noticed you demonstrating the biases you have.

➤ Complete the Circle of Trust exercise and reflect on the results. Identify what you can do to expand your circle to include people from different identity groups.

➤ Identify a Qualified Administrator of the Intercultural Development Inventory (IDI), so you can take the assessment, receive your profile and development plan, and talk with them about how you can move along the Intercultural Development Continuum (IDC).

➤ Create a Social Identity Wheel for yourself and reflect on the questions I provided earlier in the chapter. Share the results with a trusted friend, colleague, mentor, or professional coach and ask for feedback.

➤ Reflect on your privileges by first thinking about which privileges you have, both earned and unearned, and writing them down. Once you have done this, think about how they manifest themselves in your personal and professional life.

➤ Complete the cultural iceberg exercise and reflect on the questions I provided earlier. Share the results with a trusted friend, colleague, mentor, or professional coach and ask for feedback.

➤ Reflect on the eight practices you can do to manage your nervous system to better equip you to become comfortable with complexity and identify how you can develop them.

CHAPTER 5

Redressing Power Imbalances

IT WAS A WARM AND sunny day in Southern California during the latter months of the pandemic, and I was finally going to be able to meet with a longtime mentor in person. My heart was racing, as I was about to share my idea for an online course I was developing on moving from cultural competency to cultural humility. I ordered my drink and took a seat outside the coffee shop. She arrived and sat down across from me. After spending a few minutes catching up with small talk, I presented a brief overview of my course.

She looked at me with a wrinkled brow and wide eyes and said, "That's great, Joel, that you are talking about how people can improve themselves when it comes to diversity, equity, inclusion, and belonging, but so what?"

I jerked back when she asked me the question and began to stutter, as I could not find the words to respond. She took a deep breath and began to share her frustration based on her many years as a diversity consultant and educator. Her level of frustration stemmed from people who just want to focus on changing individuals but not the organization when it comes to diversity, equity, inclusion, and belonging.

As we discussed her thoughts, this point became clear: if you want to change an organization, you have to move beyond just focusing on leaders in the organization. You need to provide leaders with the necessary tools that will create the change in the organization that they want to see. She agreed personal development for leaders is the foundation, but it needs to move beyond the individuals to the organizations they lead.

In my experience, people will generally take one of two approaches when it comes to talking about the change that is needed. Consultants and coaches will usually either focus on individual change or organizational change. The reality is you need both!

That conversation with my longtime mentor was one of the catalysts for writing this book. The foundation for leading exceptionally in this area starts with you as the leader, but it needs to move beyond you. It must lead to a change in your organization. After you begin doing this work on yourself, you won't be able to resist helping other leaders and your entire organization change and develop a posture of cultural humility so the organization can create the sense of belonging everyone desires.

Putting to practice what you learned in Chapter 4 will provide the basis of beginning to lead your organization toward developing a strong sense of belonging. Just as you began with self-awareness and self-critique, you must help the organization look at itself before you can start the process of moving toward change. That process starts with identifying where power imbalances exist within the organization so you can start removing those imbalances.

Where Do the Power Imbalances in Your Organization Exist?

It was a weekday morning, and I had just gotten myself ready, had breakfast, and helped my kids get ready for school over Zoom, as we were still in the thick of the COVID-19 pandemic. I took my seat in front of my laptop in a converted corner of my bedroom that was now serving as my office. I made sure I was wearing a nice shirt, as I was about to meet with a potential consulting client. They came on and, after building rapport, I asked them how our time together would be the most helpful.

They shared that as a result of a series of race-based biased events that had happened in their organization in the aftermath of the murder of George Floyd, the company leaders had begun the work of developing a sense of belonging by initiating a series of training and development programs with the hope that their organizational climate would improve. After a few events they realized it was going to take more than just training and development to create a sense of belonging for their organization.

I asked if they had linked their efforts to their organization's mission, vision, and values. My client paused and had a confused look on their face. This was a clear indicator that they had not. My next question was, "Can you share with certainty that you know how the members of your community, particularly those from minoritized groups, are experiencing your organization?" The furrowed brow was noticeable. This response is not uncommon when it comes to leaders who want to develop the sense of belonging they desire to see in their organizations. It was clear that they didn't have a sense of *if* or *where* power imbalances exist in their organization. It is important to begin your work by linking what you are doing to your mission, vision, values. I will discuss this in more detail later in this chapter.

In Chapter 4 I covered the importance of developing self-awareness and self-critique. One of the aspects I covered was to develop other awareness. I am certain that as you begin to become familiar with the identities of those on your teams you will hear their stories and how they have experienced your organization. It is important that you, as a White leader, work to create spaces in your organization for people to share their experiences. People could share their experiences anonymously, or you could create employee resource groups.

If a team member shares with you their lived experience, you should believe them and listen to them. Then thank them for sharing this with you. A simple thank you will do, and then follow up with, "How would you like me to respond?" This gives them permission not to say anything unless they want to. These are their lived experiences, and you will certainly begin to hear where the power imbalances in your organization exist. You will feel compelled to address them.

As you hear their stories, you should also gather data that will help you see where power imbalances exist. What do I mean by gathering data? You may want to look at the current make-up of your executive team. In doing so, you may notice that everyone on your team is White and male. If you look one step down on the organizational chart you may notice the same thing. This directly impacts the direction of the organization, as your organization's leaders may not reflect the demographic make-up of the organization or the clients you serve.

As an example, you may have a high percentage of people who identify as women represented among your talent, yet most of the managers and higher-level leaders identify as men. This creates a power imbalance. Representation matters when it comes to creating a sense of belonging for everyone in your organization. Your organization may be trying to achieve this balance in its recruitment efforts, but what about retaining your talent? In looking at your talent retention data you may notice that you are losing people of color at a high rate compared to your White talent. If you do not take time to look at this data, you will not notice this imbalance.

Gathering data is a starting point in noting where power imbalances may be present so you can begin redressing the power imbalances that may exist in your organization. This will move your organization toward a posture of cultural humility. In doing this, you will begin to disrupt the usual.

You must also acknowledge that organizations were not started or created with minoritized groups in mind when it comes to your clients or your talent. You need to rethink structures within your organization, such as hiring, compensation structure, data collection and tracking, and other processes. With this awareness, you can begin to change these systems so your organization can support people outside of the dominant cultural group. Disruption is needed for this to happen.

Disrupting the Usual

If you are going to lead your organization exceptionally toward developing a strong sense of belonging, you will need to be ready to disrupt the status quo. The organization you lead was not created to support people outside of the dominant group.

A clear example is how people who are differently abled have experienced organizations. People who are differently abled have had to advocate for themselves extensively, particularly when it comes to the way buildings and offices are constructed, so they have the same access to the accommodations that able-bodied people have. Most companies were established by able-bodied people who did not have to think about the way buildings were constructed and how offices were laid out. This has started to change because organizations have been pressured to make changes to accommodate differently abled talent and clients.

The same could be said regarding race, ethnicity, and gender. Many organizations were established by White men who did not factor in people's social identities in the way they structured their organizations or the way they led their employees, leading many employees to develop a feeling of estrangement—the opposite of belonging.

It's important to revisit what I shared in Chapter 1 about belonging. Phyllis Weiss Haserot describes what belonging feels like: you are encouraged to speak up, you are taken seriously, your organization is open to curiosity and creativity, you are given psychological safety, you are not expected to be perfect, you feel welcomed in a supportive environment, and you are recognized both tangibly and intangibly for your contributions.

If these are the characteristics of what belonging feels like, then what are the characteristics of organizations that have a culture that creates estrangement? In their work *Dismantling Racism,* Kenneth Jones and Tema Okun (both activists, researchers, and educators) lay out the characteristics that make it difficult for organizations to become more inclusive and create the sense of belonging and the psychological safety they desire. These characteristics are perfectionism; sense of urgency; defensiveness; quantity over quality; worship of the written word; paternalism; either-or thinking; power hoarding; fear of open conflict; individualism; progress is bigger, more; objectivity; and right to comfort.[40]

These characteristics do not make it easy for people from minoritized groups to flourish in the organization. As I have shared earlier, this may have led your talent from these groups to feel like they do not belong and leave your organization in the hope of finding an organization that offers a stronger sense of belonging. This is a costly proposition, as stated earlier in data provided by Gallup.[41]

I have provided a way to reframe these characteristics so you can start changing your organization so it is more inclusive, radiates with a sense of belonging for everyone, and offers the crucial element of psychological safety.

- **Perfectionism** is when the expectations of your team members are so high that when a team member makes a mistake they are considered a bad person instead of what happened just being considered a mistake. Instead of giving time to reflect on the mistake that occurred to see what can be learned from it, people just move on, and the person who made the mistake might be labeled a bad team member. Another way this plays out is when organizations make their team members feel pressured to always make the right decision, which suppresses their creativity because they are more concerned about what will happen if they make the wrong decision. *Reframe:* Instead of focusing on the mistake and making the team member feel bad about what just happened, create space for reflection and make the experience an opportunity for growth. Let your talent know that you want them to experiment to find new solutions to problems and encourage them to be creative without fear of retribution.

- **Sense of urgency** is when your team members are pressured to make fast decisions with the potential for high impact, particularly when a minoritized group will be impacted. Because of the speed of decision-making, team members are not able to be inclusive by inviting diverse voices into the discussion. These organizations value quick decisions over thoughtful consideration. This could lead to missteps that may have ramifications when diverse perspectives are not sought due to the pressure to make a fast decision. As a result, the needs of minoritized groups might be sacrificed. *Reframe:* Condition your managers and leaders to give time for conversations, so diverse perspectives are included. It could be as easy as when a decision is made to ask the question: "Whose voices have we not included in our decision-making process?" Asking a question creates a moment of pause and reflection, which could combat the sense of urgency in your organizational culture.

- **Defensiveness** is when those in leadership view criticism or feedback as threatening, and talent is reprimanded in a way that stifles them from sharing ideas because those in leadership roles view new ideas as a threat to their leadership. This creates a culture where talent spends time and energy figuring out how to get around people to share ideas. *Reframe:* Providing training in the form of workshops and mentoring will help your leaders learn that new ideas should be valued and not seen as threatening. Help leaders work on their need to be defensive and to be open to people's ideas regardless of their position in the organization.

- **Quantity over quality** looks like when your organization uses its resources to produce things that can be measured quantifiably, and it is highly valued to operate in this way. No one spends time evaluating what the process to achieve this goal looks like and the impact it has on your talent. For example: "We produce 1,000 widgets a day, even if it means the entire team works at breakneck speed day and night, including weekends." This characteristic stifles your talent from being able to share ideas or how these decisions are impacting their well-being. *Reframe:* Create goals for quality that are valued as highly as those for quantity. If one of your goals is for your organization to become more inclusive (a qualitative goal) you could develop key performance indicators to measure if the goal is being achieved. This will mean asking talent about how they feel and what changes they would like to see so people's ideas are valued and your organization will continue to become more inclusive.

- **Worship of the written word** is when your organization places a high value on putting things in writing and does not consider other forms of communication. For example, for some of the talent in your organization, English may be their second language. This may mean that articulating ideas in writing does not come easily to them, making it hard for them to feel like their opinions are valued. This could translate as your organization only sees putting things in writing in the dominant language as the only way to communicate. *Reframe:* There are many ways to communicate that need to be acknowledged and valued. There is not one right way, and just because someone on the team cannot articulate an idea well in writing does not mean they do not have good ideas. You may want to provide opportunities for your talent to share ideas verbally. This could mean holding town hall forums or conducting group sessions with talent, particularly those from minoritized communities, so they can share their thoughts. This will allow those who may not be able to express ideas in writing to feel valued and seen, particularly team members who may come from cultures that place a high value on the spoken word.

- **Paternalism** is when people in the organization are unclear who has the decision-making power, but those in power know exactly who has the power to make decisions. Those with decision-making power do not make an effort to involve those who do not have decision-making power. Those without power do not know how decisions are made or who makes those decisions, but they directly feel the impact of those decisions. *Reframe:* Leaders must articulate who has decision-making power and how decisions are made. They need to include people who may have been traditionally excluded from the decision-making process, like talent from minoritized communities, so those impacted by decisions have an opportunity to share their perspective and what the impact of decisions will be.

- **Either-or thinking** is when organizations and leaders think of things as good or bad, right or wrong, us versus them—all examples of either-or thinking—instead of both-and thinking. This can lead to oversimplifying complex problems; for example, the cause of people being unhoused is simply because they don't want to get jobs. It leads to minimizing people's experiences in the organization and making them feel "less than." It also leads to conflict, as decisions may be rushed instead of exploring multiple perspectives. An example could be a view that women in the organization just need to work harder if they want to get paid more, or new professionals just need to pay their dues before their ideas can be heard. *Reframe:* When leaders observe either-or thinking, ask questions that can lead to deeper conversations. For example, they could ask for more than two alternatives to problems that are complex, especially when the stakes may be high. In the example I shared earlier, it could look like asking for a deeper analysis when it comes to pay equity and transparency.

- **Power hoarding** is when power sharing does not exist in the organization. Leaders use a scarcity mindset when it comes to how many people can make a decision in the organization. People in the organization with the power to make decisions do not realize that they are hoarding, or they feel threatened by sharing their authority. They also view people who want their power to be shared as just not understanding or that they do not have the same experience they do and, therefore, are incapable of making the decision. *Reframe:*

Clearly articulate in writing how authority to make decisions will be distributed and shared. This will demonstrate for people the value of shared leadership. Have a conversation with leaders about what exceptional leadership looks like and the expectations that the organization has for shared decision-making.

- **Fear of open conflict** is when people in the organization shy away from conflict and confrontation for fear of feeling uneasy. It could also mean leaders dismiss the conflict using either-or thinking or because they do not want to explore the source of the conflict. If someone raises an issue, they might be labeled as malcontent or not adhering to the line of command. *Reframe:* Spend time developing a culture where conflict is seen as a growth opportunity and clarify how conflict is handled before conflict arises. Stress the importance of not being dismissive of those who raise an issue that leads to conflict.

- **Individualism** is when people in the organization do not see the value of working with others and make no effort to work with others. The organization places a high value on competition and rewards it by recognizing those in the organization who clearly do not work well with others. Cooperation with others is seen as a waste of time and team members are not given the time and resources needed to develop the skills to work as a team. *Reframe:* Develop a system where people are rewarded for working with others and developing their team, so they can better accomplish organizational goals. For example, your organization could create a bonus structure that rewards ideas generated in groups versus in isolation.

- **Progress is bigger, more** is when an organization places a high value on growth and expansion without factoring in the impact this has on people. A common mantra is that people must do more with less, and if they can't they are shown the door. *Reframe:* Create space for people to discuss the impact the growth will have on talent, not just on the financial statement. More specifically, leaders should discuss the impact the growth could have on the organization's morale or what the impact could be many years down the road.

- **Objectivity** is when an organization does not acknowledge that situations can be nuanced or that people's biases may play a role in how they make decisions. Leaders dismiss anything they perceive as not being objective and think it should not be factored into the decision-making process. If people show emotion, they are told their emotions are impacting their ability to remain objective and logical rather than exploring their emotions as a potential way to look at something differently.

Reframe: Acknowledge that your team brings multiple perspectives to the table and that their perspectives can impact how decisions are made and provide a new way of thinking. Leaders need to seek to understand people's different viewpoints and not be so quick to dismiss their viewpoints as not objective and, therefore, not valuable.

- **Right to comfort** is a perspective that those in leadership need to remain comfortable and that anyone who threatens their comfort has a problem and needs to change, not the leaders. *Reframe:* Help leaders become comfortable with being uncomfortable. This could take the form of facilitating conversations to help people understand that discomfort is part of any growth process. Help leaders deepen their understanding of the people they lead by learning more about their identities and their lived experiences.

Not all these characteristics may apply to your organization, and some may be manifesting themselves in subtle ways. Some may show up in various areas of the organization due to the respective managers' leadership styles. It is important that you help your organization look at itself in the mirror to determine which of these are showing up. This may include asking people in your organization whom you believe can provide a critical view that will be necessary to determine if your organization has a sense of belonging. This could be as simple as including questions in your next organizational engagement survey and then looking at the results from the survey by demographic groups (for example, women, people of color, age group, and so forth).

You may think some of these characteristics are good things, and you may value some of them. I would challenge you to identify someone in your organization who does not share the same identities as you and ask them how they feel when they hear these characteristics. This will be a heavy lift, but one that will go a long way to identify and redress the power imbalances that may exist. You may want to start by taking some time to reflect on each of these characteristics and conduct an organizational assessment to determine if they exist in your organization.

The work of identifying these characteristics that create estrangement in your organization, then taking the steps to change them, will make many people feel uncomfortable, as they are accustomed to the status quo and will not want things to change because it creates discomfort. You will encounter people who say they just want things to go back to the way they were. Another way to put this is that they will feel nostalgic. This is common, but nostalgia needs to be evaluated from multiple perspectives.

The "way things were" included not allowing women to use company credit cards and not giving them senior-level roles because of a belief that woman could not manage finances well, fear they would get pregnant and quit, or because they were labeled as too emotional. People of color were not considered for senior-level roles because companies were concerned they did not have the right "look" for an executive, meaning their skin color was too dark, and White men were preferred because they looked the part of an executive leader. People who identified as openly gay were not considered for roles for fear of contracting AIDS or they were not "man enough."

When you encounter people in the organization who say they want to go back to the "way things were" remind them about how things were for people from minoritized groups. You could preface the DEIB work you are doing by referencing how things once were and stressing the positive outcomes that will come from changing the organization's culture. This will give them something to think about and help them realize the power imbalances that are being exposed need to be addressed in order for your organization to make progress and create the sense of belonging it wants to actualize. This will help your organization attract and retain talent at a high rate and meet the needs of your diverse clients.

You want to lead exceptionally, and this means helping your organization move from an organization that just promotes equality to one that promotes equity. You may be wondering what the difference is between equality and equity. It's important to understand the difference, because there is a difference.

Equality versus Equity

Equality is when a person or group of people are provided with the same resources or opportunities that everyone has. *Equity* is recognition that each person has different circumstances and is given specific resources and opportunities to get to an equal outcome. Becoming an equitable organization will go a long way to create the sense of belonging you wish to establish. It will require your organization to look at the data to determine if equity exists; for example, the way it recruits, promotes, provides professional development opportunities, and compensates talent.

If your organization makes equity a priority and you determine that a certain population in your talent pool is not as successful as the people in the majority population in your workforce, you will need to create initiatives to help the identified group move toward success at a level that matches the majority population. For example, if you determine that your Latino employees are leaving your organization at a higher rate than your White employees, you will create programs that specifically target your Latino employees so you move toward retaining them at the same rate as your White employees. This is moving toward creating equity.

You may also determine in your research that your organization's leadership needs to be developed so they understand the unique challenges your Latino employees are facing and can adjust their leadership style to meet the needs of the Latinos in your organization. You may also need to adjust some of your policies based on what you discover in your research about why your Latino talent pool is leaving at a higher rate. This means you will need to remove barriers to retaining your Latino talent so you can achieve equity for this population in your workforce.

You are probably thinking that this won't fly with your human resources department. That may be the case, so you may want to get creative in the approach you take to work toward achieving equity. This will require getting the right people around the table and possibly partnering with a coach or consultant to help you identify and implement ways to become a more equitable organization. All this work will require linking your efforts with your organization's mission, vision, and values—without this connection your efforts will fail under the pressure from people who do not believe what you are doing is right or justified.

Tying DEIB to Your Mission, Vision, and Values

Connecting your diversity, equity, inclusion, and belonging efforts to your mission, vision, and values will be the foundation for your organization to begin making the changes necessary to becoming a more inclusive organization that has a strong sense of belonging. Earlier in this chapter I shared my conversation with my potential client and how I asked them if they were linking their efforts to their mission, vision, and values. I cannot stress enough the importance of connecting your efforts to these guiding beliefs and statements. You need to start by reviewing your current mission, vision, and values. What do they say about your organization? Do they articulate your desire to serve a diverse client base? Do they communicate that you want your organization to foster a sense of belonging, so talent from minoritized groups feel like they belong?

In this section I will share three examples of organizations that have clearly articulated that they are making diversity, equity, inclusion, and belonging a priority.

Your organization has more than likely done a lot of work to identify its mission, vision, and values like a lot of other organizations. Why? Because leadership knows that clearly articulating these beliefs and statements guides an organization toward achieving its goals. Organizations that do this exceptionally well can meet their financial goals and distinguish themselves from their competitors. This leads to meeting the needs of their clients more effectively and recruiting the type of talent they want at their organization.

Here are three examples of organizational statements that make diversity, equity, inclusion, and belonging a stated priority. It is important to note that these are examples and not an endorsement of these organizations.

- **General Motors,** an automotive company, has made it clear on its website that this global organization is making inclusion a priority by clearly stating the following: "We aspire to be the world's most inclusive company and to conduct ourselves with fairness and transparency toward everyone we interact with."[42] This public statement goes on to list eight behaviors, one of which is being inclusive.

- **Asana,** a project management software company, makes it clear that it is committed to DEIB by stating: "We believe in teams. Yours and ours. Our mission, culture, and commitment to fostering a diverse, inclusive workplace lets us build a product people love and stay true to ourselves."[43] This statement clearly articulates that diversity, equity, inclusion, and belonging are important to this organization.

- **Humana,** a health care company, makes the following statement about why diversity, equity, inclusion, and belonging are important to the entire organization and beyond: "At Humana, we focus on making it easy for each person to achieve whole-person health and well-being. We're proud of the work we do day in and day out in caring for people. When we say we want to make living a healthy life easier for everyone, we truly mean it for our members, for our associates, and for you. We also recognize that we are part of a bigger community and are dedicated to the well-being of all people. That is why we invest in communities across the country to advance health equity, which is about making sure we all have a fair and just opportunity to be as healthy as possible. Helping communities and the people in them grow stronger benefits all of us because where people live, work and play are inextricable from their health outcomes."[44] This is a clear example of what is important to this organization and why its leaders believe it's important to create an inclusive organization.

As an organization you will need to spend time articulating why your desire to create a strong sense of belonging is important. It is not enough to just put it in writing—as with any mission, vision, and values statement, you must put it into action. The organizations I listed have taken the first step toward creating organizations that are inclusive and have a strong sense of belonging. They need to build on the strong foundation they have created. You will need to do the same.

In this chapter I discussed the importance of identifying and redressing the power imbalances that exist in your organization. I also highlighted the importance of starting with your mission, vision, and values if you are going change your organization into what you desire it to look like. The next step will require additional intentionality and will need exceptional leadership to move your organization forward.

To move your organization toward becoming inclusive and having a strong sense of belonging, you will need to have a framework to guide your efforts or you run the risk of just creating programs that may look good but do not actually lead to the change you are seeking. This is where many organizations fail! They do not monitor their efforts to ensure they are making progress. Having a framework will help you make sure you don't just create a laundry list of initiatives that look good but do not actually make a difference.

Here is a tool that will help guide your efforts: the Dimensions of Diversity framework. Originally developed by the educator, researcher, and diversity consultant Dr. Daryl G. Smith, her framework consisted of four dimensions for institutions of higher education.

I have taken those dimensions and changed their labels so they can apply to all types of organizations. They are organizational vitality and viability, organizational climate and intergroup relations, training and development, and recruitment and engagement. In the next chapter, I will go into detail on each of these dimensions. This framework will be vital in moving your organization toward becoming more inclusive and having the strong sense of belonging you desire it to have.

Take Action

> Take time now to answer the following question: What power imbalances currently exist in your organization? If you don't know the answer, what do you need to do to find the answer?

> Think back to the feelings associated with a sense of belonging (you are encouraged to speak up, you are taken seriously, your organization is open to curiosity and creativity, you are given psychological safety, you are not expected to be perfect, you feel welcomed in a supportive environment, and you are recognized both tangibly and intangibly for your contributions). Are these feelings you would associate with your organization? Why or why not?

> Think back to the characteristics associated with organizations that do not foster a sense of belonging (perfectionism; sense of urgency; defensiveness; quantity over quality; worship of the written word; paternalism; either-or thinking; power hoarding; fear of open conflict; individualism; progress is bigger, more; objectivity; and the right to comfort). Which of these characteristics does your organization demonstrate? Identify people in your organization with whom you can share the list to get an honest assessment from someone else.

➤ List your current initiatives that are related to DEIB. Then answer the following question: How are they connected to your mission, vision, and values? If they are not, why not? What steps can you take to connect them?

CHAPTER 6

Change Systems to Be More Inclusive

MY EYELIDS FELT HEAVY, I had just grabbed my morning cup of coffee. I was sitting in my chair located in what was now my office in the corner of my bedroom, waiting for a call from a longtime colleague and friend. It was at the height of the pandemic, and I was doing what many of us did during that time—reaching out to friends and colleagues to reconnect. My colleague had just left to take on another role at an organization, and we were going to catch up. I dialed his number, and he picked up. After spending some time catching up and reminiscing about our times at our previous organization where I had served as the chief diversity officer, he paused. His pause seemed out of place, and I was not sure what he was about to say.

"I want to thank you, Joel," he said.

Now it was my turn to pause. "You're welcome," I said. "For what?"

He shared his reflections about his time at our previous organization. Specifically, he was thankful for the work I had undertaken to help create a more inclusive organization. He wanted me to know that my work was instrumental in helping him and other colleagues from minoritized communities feel like they belonged and that my work had fundamentally changed the organization. I thanked him and shared that the work was a heavy lift but well worth the effort.

After we hung up, I reflected on my time as the chief diversity officer for that organization, remembering how important it was to have a framework to guide the effort and the work I led as a senior leader. Our discussion reminded me about how I felt before I started leading these efforts. I felt like many leaders do, that this initiative was virtually impossible given the nature of diversity work. I then remembered how it felt as we started laying out the plan to change the organization and put the systems in place. That feeling was one of accomplishment as the changes we were making led to transformation. In turn, this led to people feeling like they belonged.

I share this story so you know that it is possible to lead efforts that will lead to organizational change and to people feeling like they belong. Specifically, people will feel like they are able to speak up and be listened to, be taken seriously, be open to curiosity, given psychological safety, not expected to be perfect, feel welcomed, and be recognized for their contributions. This is what my friend was describing in our conversation.

As discussed, some characteristics can get in the way of organizations developing a sense of belonging, which leads to feelings of estrangement and an absence of psychological safety. Those characteristics are perfectionism; sense of urgency; defensiveness; quantity over quality; worship of the written word; paternalism; either-or thinking; power hoarding; fear of open conflict; individualism; progress is bigger, more; objectivity; and the right to comfort. In the previous chapter I shared how to positively reframe these harmful characteristics that prevent organizations from developing a deep sense of belonging so you can change the narrative.

What else gets in the way of organizations making changes necessary to becoming more inclusive and having a sense of belonging? These issues can lead organizations' efforts to fail or not achieve their goals: not having exceptional leaders in place; not linking your efforts to your mission, vision, and values; not having a framework to guide your efforts or identifying indicators that will mark your impact and success. As I shared in Chapter 4, it starts with you, and it starts by developing the self-awareness and self-critique that will lead you toward developing a posture of cultural humility. You need to start working on yourself first! If you do not, your ability to lead exceptionally in creating the change you want to see will not work.

The work of developing this posture is an ongoing effort and not a box to check. So, if you think you need to have it all together to start changing your organization, you are mistaken! It starts with changing yourself and then turning your attention toward the organization you lead. These two activities can happen simultaneously.

The work of changing your organization must start with

identifying and choosing a framework to guide your efforts. As I mentioned in the previous chapter, I have used with success the Dimensions of Diversity framework developed by Dr. Daryl G. Smith.[45] As you can see in Figure 5, those Dimensions of Diversity are organizational vitality and viability, recruitment and engagement, training and development, and organizational climate and intergroup relations.

The following paragraphs describe the framework and how you can use it. Using this framework will lead to your organization to become more inclusive and develop the sense of belonging you wish to create.

ORGANIZATIONAL INDICATORS

Organizational
Vitality & Viability

Training &
Development

ORGANIZATIONAL
MISSION

Recruitment &
Engagement

Organizational
Climate &
Intergoup Relations

Figure 5. Dimensions of Diversity Framework

Dimensions of Diversity Framework

The development of this framework came from documenting the history of diversity in American higher education. More specifically, early on institutions focused on recruiting more students from minoritized groups (recruitment and engagement)—think the 1960s to 1970s. The focus then turned to the interactions students were having with each other (organizational climate and intergroup relations) in the 1980s. During the 1990s the focus moved toward what was being taught and how it was taught (training and development), and finally in the early 2000s what the institution was doing to make deep and lasting change (organizational vitality and viability). Ultimately, it became clear that institutions of higher learning needed to change to better meet the needs of a changing society. Dr. Daryl G. Smith[46] developed a framework, which provided a roadmap that helps organizations think about how they can change and guide their diversity, equity, inclusion, and belonging efforts. It also provides a way to measure and track progress over time. It is imperative that organizations utilize a framework to guide and monitor their efforts, track progress, and measure the impact of the initiatives they are implementing for the desired change being sought.

A metaphor that can be helpful is the work that many organizations undertook (and continue to undertake) when integrating technology into their organizations. Organizations face many challenges when it comes to integrating technology, but we would not think of an organization being able to function without technology to meet the needs of its clients and talent. For example, adopting a new client relations management (CRM) system takes time and resources, but ultimately it will lead to serving clients better and having a good return on investment.

The same goes for the work needed for organizations to be more inclusive and have a sense of belonging. Both take a lot of work and investment in leadership and financial commitments, and both will have a positive impact on how you serve your stakeholders. The amount of work that organizations put into developing their ability to integrate technology is the same amount of work that is needed to be more inclusive, but the results can be even more profound, leading to change within yourself, your organization, and the broader community.

If I were guiding your organization through this process, I would start with presenting and describing the framework, so you would understand the value of having a framework to guide your efforts and gain an understanding of each of the dimensions. Once your organization understands the dimensions, I would work with you to identify a baseline for each of the dimensions so you can begin to determine how your organization is currently doing within each dimension. Having a baseline would help you assess where you are currently so you can determine where gaps may exist and can redress the power imbalances that I described in Chapter 5. You would then be able to develop goals to redress the power imbalances.

The second step would be to develop a list of indicators that would identify what success looks like for each of the dimensions. Indicators can be specific to your organization, meaning the type and industry. The key is to identify indicators that would indicate if you are being successful in each dimension. They would ensure that you know you are making progress toward developing an inclusive organization and a strong sense of belonging. The indicators would also help you identify the types of initiatives to put in place so you can achieve the indicators. You would want to spend time thinking through initiatives that would be appropriate for your organization based on your industry.

The third and final step would be to identify the initiatives that you believe would lead to meeting the indicators for success. The following paragraphs describe each of the Dimensions of Diversity and present questions to consider when identifying a baseline, potential indicators for success for each dimension, and possible initiatives your organization may want to implement to achieve the identified indicators. As a reminder, the four Dimensions of Diversity are organizational vitality and viability, recruitment and engagement, training and development, and organizational climate and intergroup relations.

Dimension 1: Organizational Vitality and Viability

The focus of this dimension is on what your organization is doing to build the capacity and structures for diversity so your organization can sustain its efforts over time. It describes your organization's ability to plan, implement, coordinate, and assess its diversity, equity, inclusion, and belonging efforts. It also describes your organization's human, organizational, and fiscal resources needed to support DEIB efforts. Examples might include human and institutional resources dedicated to diversity, equity, inclusion, and belonging. Are you aligning your work with your mission, vision, and values? As I shared earlier, this is central so that you anchor your work. If you miss this, then you will easily lose your focus. In the process of aligning your work you may discover that your mission, vision, and values need to be modified so you can align your efforts to them.

Potential questions to determine a baseline: What is your current budget related to your DEIB efforts? What is the current composition of your executive team regarding their identities? This question will lead to a conversation about what your organization wants to include in the definition of compositional diversity. This might include race/ethnicity, gender, LGBTQ+, and so forth. It will be important to define what you mean by *compositional diversity* before you identify the baseline as well as other targets related to the other dimensions. Other baseline questions might include: What are your current staffing levels related to DEIB? What statements do you have related to your commitment as an organization to DEIB?

Potential indicators: A key indicator is the centrality of DEIB in the organization's mission, vision, and values. For example, are your efforts clearly articulated in your mission, vision, and values? Also consider integrating DEIB into the organizational strategic planning process as well as improving the compositional diversity of your executive team, senior leadership, and management. This could be setting a target to increase the percentage of those who identify as women on your executive team, those who identify as people of color, and so forth. For example, clarifying this indicator could lead to a commitment to increase the composition in the next three years by 10 percent of people of color or 20 percent of those who identify as women. Another potential indicator you may decide on is the public's perception of the organization's commitment to DEIB. If your organization conducts a client/customer survey, you can include a question about their perception of your commitment to DEIB in the survey. Once you collect that data you can then break it up by demographic category to determine how each group views your organization.

Potential initiatives: Start by linking your organization's mission, vision, and values to the work you are doing in the area of DEIB. Other options include establishing a chief diversity officer position, creating a compelling story about the work you are doing and sharing it with stakeholders, hiring people in senior leadership positions who reflect multiple identities, and developing and sharing a statement that communicates your commitment.

Dimension 2: Recruitment and Engagement

The focus of this dimension is on hiring talent and keeping them at all levels of the organization. This means looking at entry-level, mid-level, and senior-level positions in the organization. When doing work in this dimension, organizations look at the demographics of talent at all levels. The focus is not only on what you are doing to hire a more diverse talent pool, but also what are you doing to engage your talent so you retain them. This is the dimension that many organizations begin with and traditionally has been the focus of diversity, equity, inclusion, and belonging efforts, but it takes more than hiring for diversity for an organization to be more inclusive or produce a sense of belonging.

Potential questions to determine a baseline: What is the current percentage of people from minoritized groups in your applicant pool for your positions at all levels (entry-level, mid-level, and senior-level)? What is your current talent retention rate for minoritized talent at every level? It is important that you break up this information by each group so you can see where gaps may exist.

Potential indicators: Look at the level of engagement of your talent broken up by the groups you are trying to improve retention with, compared to the retention rate of your talent at all levels. For example, if your organization has mid-level managers, what percentage of this group continues to stay at your organization from year to year? This could vary depending on your industry; you will need to work with your HR department to determine the baseline and a realistic percentage to try to meet on an annual basis. An additional indicator to consider is the leadership advancement in the organization of your talent pool broken up by minoritized groups. For example, do your Asian American employees advance through the leadership ranks at the same rate as your White employees?

Potential initiatives: Ideas include hiring talent at all levels from minoritized communities, working to ensure their success, and measuring and tracking the level of engagement of your minoritized talent. This could be done by analyzing the data you collect when you conduct employee engagement surveys. It could also include creating a plan to establish metrics to recruit talent from minoritized communities.

Dimension 3: Training and Development

The focus of this dimension is on building the capacity of your talent to foster an inclusive community and a sense of belonging in your organizational culture. It involves improving the way you onboard your talent and structure your ongoing professional development so your talent can lead exceptionally, leading to a more inclusive organization.

Potential questions to determine a baseline: What are the components of your onboarding process related to DEIB? For example, do you provide training for your new managers when it comes to identifying and mitigating the impact that bias has on the hiring process? Other questions might be: What are the components of the learning and development program related to DEIB? What percentage of each of them are related to DEIB?

Potential indicators: Determine if you are providing ongoing training to your talent to build their capacity to successfully engage in DEIB, the type of support you are providing your talent from minoritized groups, and the percentage of components in your onboarding process related to DEIB.

Potential initiatives: Consider identifying and implementing a professional development program that will increase the capacity of your workforce to develop their skill set in DEIB. For example, you could provide workshops so your talent can learn how to develop their cultural self-awareness by utilizing the Intercultural Development Inventory. Another initiative could be implementing an employee resource group to support your talent from minoritized communities.

Dimension 4: Organizational Climate and Intergroup Relations

The focus of this dimension is assessing your organization's climate so you can determine the experience your talent is having. It's also about looking at how your team members are experiencing each other. You are looking at the type and quality of social interactions among your talent as well as your clients' perceptions of your organization's commitment to diversity, equity, inclusion, and belonging.

Potential questions to determine a baseline: What are the experiences of your talent in your organization related to DEIB? This could be determined by analyzing data from an employee engagement survey or by conducting focus groups. What are the types and qualities of the interaction that your employees are having with each other?

Potential indicators: Take a close look at the type and quality of interaction among groups in your organization broken up by demographic group, perceptions of your organization's commitment and engagement of DEIB broken up demographic group, and the level of engagement in your organization broken up by demographic group.

Potential initiatives: Consider conducting an organizational climate study to determine the type of experience everyone within the organization is having broken up by demographic groups. You could also establish a communication plan to share with stakeholders (both internal and external) about your success and challenges in achieving your goals, establish a bias incident response protocol with a mechanism to ensure accountability, and develop a plan to turn critical incidents into opportunities to improve organizational climate and facilitate learning.

The goal is to work toward addressing each of these dimensions. You cannot just focus on one, as they are all interrelated and build on each other. The temptation may be just to focus on one at a time; that is the wrong approach, as they are symbiotic.

Developing a plan using the Dimensions of Diversity will be instrumental in helping your organization become more inclusive and develop that sense of belonging you are hoping to create. It does not end with this work. Having a plan, indicators, and initiatives is the starting point. As with any organizational strategic plan, you will need to track and monitor progress if you are going to learn from what is taking place and make the adjustments necessary to keep making progress. This framework is predicated on using data to guide your efforts. What do I mean by that?

In a *Harvard Business Review* article titled "How to Best Use Data to Meet Your DEI Goals,"[47] authors Siri Chilazi and Iris Bohnet[48] noted the fact that tech companies Google, Facebook, Apple, and Microsoft shared the data on their diversity efforts, which served as an excellent motivator for them to make progress toward their organizational goals. Why? Because it created the accountability needed to ensure they were trying meet their goals. The authors shared four insights from their research: present diversity data in a way that is easy to understand; leverage the data to motivate key people in the organization to act; set goals to provide accountability; and harness the data to move social norms around diversity, equity, inclusion, and belonging.

The reality is that if you are going to be successful in initiating, implementing, and coordinating change you must use data to monitor and track your progress. You won't know if the initiatives you have implemented are creating the change you desire unless you monitor, track, and report the data. As I shared earlier in this chapter, it starts with identifying a baseline. For example, if you want to hire more talent from the identified target groups, you need to first

find out where you are so you can establish a goal you want
to pursue. An example might be that if your current workforce only has 10 percent representation of people of color
and you want to increase that to 25 percent in the next three
years, you probably need to develop an aggressive plan that
will mean putting resources into identifying, hiring, and
successfully onboarding the talent. Another example could
be that in identifying a baseline you come to realize that you
are losing 15 percent of your talent who identify as LGBTQ+
per year compared to a smaller percentage of those who do
not identity as LGBTQ+. If you want to decrease that percentage to 5 percent over the next three years, you know you
need to create and implement initiatives that will improve
their engagement in your organization.

It's not only important to know the data, but it is also
important for you to share the data with your stakeholders.
Transparency is key if you are going to build trust and show
that you are making or not making progress. For example,
as part of your annual meeting you could provide an update
on the progress or the lack of progress you are making. If
you are not making progress and you can see that in the
data, you can then develop interventions to help you move
the needle in the right direction.

Peter Senge, in his book *The Fifth Discipline: The Art and
Practice of the Learning Organization,*[49] stresses the importance of creating feedback loops so organizations can ana-
lyze data in real time and make the adjustments necessary
to successfully implement the change they want to see.
Implementing change in the areas of diversity, equity, inclusion, and belonging is no different. What is the baseline for
the type of change you want to see in your organization?

You want to start the work by identifying the baseline, as this will directly influence the goals you set to achieve the change you want to see.

Let's see what this process looks like in action. Over the years in my role as a chief diversity officer and consultant I have worked with organizations that have successfully developed a plan using the Dimensions of Diversity framework. Here is what that looked like.

Organizational Example

I was serving as the chief diversity officer for an organization that was trying to become more inclusive and develop a sense of belonging but did not know where to begin. I was promoted to a senior-level position, and I knew immediately that we needed a plan that would take the organization from good intentions to sustainable change.

I began by introducing the Dimensions of Diversity framework to the organization and gained approval to move forward with this framework to guide the process. I then composed the group that would develop the plan. Bringing the right people together is the first step and will be key, as you want to make sure you bring a collaborative group of people together. The proverb "many hands make light work" is applicable when working toward creating an inclusive organization. You cannot do this work on your own. You will need to identify people in your organization who can work with you.

In his book *Leading Change,*[50] John P. Kotter stresses the importance of creating a guiding coalition. He states, "Because major change is so difficult to accomplish, a powerful force is required to sustain the process. No one individual, even a monarch-like CEO, is ever able to develop the right vision, communicate it to large numbers of people, eliminate all the key obstacles, generate short-term wins, lead and manage dozens of change projects, and anchor new approaches deep in the organization's culture." He goes on to describe four key characteristics needed in a guiding coalition:

1. **Position power:** You want key organizational members on your team. This will include people with influence and positional power.
2. **Expertise:** You want team members who have a good understanding of DEIB.
3. **Credibility:** You want people with a good reputation in the organization.
4. **Leadership:** You want team members who have the proven leadership to lead the change effort.

These are the characteristics you will need to consider when composing your guiding coalition. You should spend time thinking of who you will want on your team.

I was able to bring together the right group of people to create the plan. We then followed the process that I described earlier in the chapter. Along the way we learned that, as with any change initiative, some people in the organization will resist change. As I led the effort to create the plan, I spent a lot of time with people who were resistant to the change. I believed I could convince them that this work was important. Based on my experience and subsequent work as a consultant I realize this was a mistake! I now know I was experiencing the innovation adoption cycle.[51]

The innovation adoption cycle describes how people receive change when they are first presented with it. It was introduced by Everett Rogers and his colleagues in 1957. The theory states that 2.5 percent of the people will be *innovators* of the change; I propose changing *innovators* to *early champions* of the change being sought. These are the people who will be allies and advocates of the change your organization is pursuing. The theory then states that 13.5 percent of the people will be *early adopters* of the change. These are the people whom you will not have to convince; they will be in from the beginning. The next 34 percent will be the *early majority*. With this group you will have to do some level of convincing that this change is necessary, but they will not need a lot of convincing. The next 34 percent are referred to as the *late majority*. These people will need more convincing but will ultimately adopt the change. The last 16 percent are referred to as *laggards*. These people may come around but most likely will only come "kicking and screaming."

In my work as an organizational change leader, I advise organizations and leaders to focus their attention on the 68 percent in the middle (the early majority and the late majority). You will need a strategy to move them along, but ultimately, if done well, they will come around and embrace the change. The tendency is for leaders to focus on the laggards, and this was what I did. I realize now that this group will suck up your energy, creating unnecessary anxiety and stress. Make the middle group your focus, and the laggards may come along. If they don't, well that is their choice, and it may be time to release them to their future, because they are not committed to the work that needs to be done.

After I developed my strategy on how I would use the framework to guide my organization's effort, I started thinking about the people in the organization and where they may land on the innovation adoption cycle as it related to the change process. You are probably starting to do the same thing. This is important and will be helpful as you develop a strategy to initiate the change you want to see in your organization.

After the plan was completed and adopted, I then moved to operationalize it. This included developing the budget for each of the initiatives we identified to help us meet the indicators and the timeline associated with each initiative.

It was vitally important that the team continued to meet to track and monitor the progress. This meant developing key performance indicators for each of the indicators. For example, we started tracking the retention rate for each of the demographic groups we had identified where we wanted to improve the retention rate. This helped us make sure we were making progress, and if we discovered we were not moving the needle in the right direction, we were quick to develop a strategy to get on track.

This was also key: I provided an update a year into the plan to demonstrate the progress to organizational leaders that we were making and where we still had work to do. This kept the key stakeholders informed and held us accountable for the work we were doing. All this work led to the change my colleague described in the story I shared earlier and the impact that this process had in creating the sense of belonging that led to a more inclusive organization. Although I did not see the change happening as we were doing the work, it paid dividends down the road, even after I left the organization.

The process from start to finish took about eighteen months to complete, but the result led to creating momentum for the organization to move toward becoming more inclusive and having a sense of belonging as demonstrated by my opening story. That momentum still exists to this day. The time it takes for your organization to complete this process from start to finish will vary depending on the type of organization and the existing culture. Based on my experience, if you do a good job getting the right people in the room and have the organizational commitment from senior leadership and your board, you are extremely likely to be successful. This approach and commitment, in combination with having a posture of cultural humility, will help you achieve the change you want to see in your organization.

The work you are starting, if done well, will live beyond a person or a program. It will become part of the ethos of the organization, leading to deep and lasting change, just as the move organizations make when adopting technology. It also means the work will need to continue and requires resources to ensure that it continues. If it does not get the resources necessary, it will fade out, and your organization will be back to where it started. The key is that you make the investment necessary to become more inclusive and create the sense of belonging you desire for your organization. If you are able to create the momentum necessary, the change you will achieve will have ripple effects for you, your organization, and the community. The next chapter describes what that impact will be.

Take Action

Now that you've completed this chapter, take a moment to reflect on the questions below in relation to your organization. Utilize the answers to these questions to build your Dimensions of Diversity strategy.

➤ How have you aligned your DEIB efforts to your mission, vision, and values? If you have not, why? What is holding you back?

➤ How are you actively tracking the demographics of your talent for all levels?

➤ How are you including topics of DEIB in your talent development and onboarding program?

➤ What is your organization doing to measure the climate and intergroup interactions?

➤ What current initiatives does your organization have related to DEIB, and if you were going to categorize them using the framework, where would you place them?

➤ How are you using data to guide your DEIB efforts?

CHAPTER 7

Impact on Yourself, Your Organization, and Your Community

THE PROCESS OF DEVELOPING A posture of cultural humility begins with you, but it does not stop there. In Chapter 4 I laid out how you can begin to develop a posture of cultural humility, and that it will take time, but that you must get started to get where you want to go. I also shared that this needs to be bigger than you. Working toward developing a posture of cultural humility will make you the exceptional leader you desire to be and will lead to you creating the change in the organization you serve to be more inclusive and have a sense of belonging.

To illustrate this point, picture an orchestra. An orchestra is composed of individuals who are talented musicians and have spent years developing their artistic skills, but it does not stop with just being a beginning or even an intermediate musician. Musicians who want to be exceptional must continue to develop themselves so they can contribute to the success of the orchestra. Similarly, you will not be able to make substantive changes on your own; you will need a community of leaders to help you on your journey. Like an orchestra member, you need others to help you produce music. You will need to identify people who can journey with you as you develop and lead with a posture of cultural humility. A pivotal person on your team can be a mentor or a coach.

The impact you will have on the organization as you develop this posture can be compared to the conductor's impact on the orchestra. As I described in Chapter 5, you will begin to see where the power imbalances reside in your organization and work toward redressing those imbalances. This is like a conductor who will notice where an instrumentalist needs to play louder or more consistently with the orchestra, so the whole is achieving its goal of harmonizing and producing the music the conductor and musicians desire to produce.

The posture of cultural humility you are developing will have an immense impact on the organization, helping it to achieve its mission, vision, and values. Becoming more inclusive and creating a deep sense of belonging will meet the needs of your talent so you can attract and retain them. In Chapter 6 I shared with you the Dimensions of Diversity framework that will lead your organization toward becoming more inclusive and developing a sense of belonging. I stressed the importance of using a framework to guide your efforts so you can show that the work you are doing is having an impact and achieving the goal of becoming more inclusive and having a sense of belonging.

In addition, by developing a posture of cultural humility you will have an impact on the community. Just as an orchestra has an impact on the audience that has assembled to hear the music, you and your organization will have an impact on the community. In your case, as the exceptional leader, this impact will be felt around the dinner table and in conversations with your family, your faith community, and the volunteer roles you serve in. In the case of the organization, the impact will be felt in the community, both the local community and the professional community.

When you develop a posture of cultural humility you will see a ripple effect. Let me share how developing a posture of cultural humility will be felt by those around you when you apply it outside of your organizational context, starting with its impact on you, the individual.

The Impact on You, as an Individual

I had a smile on my face and was light on my feet. My old college roommate had come to visit me and my family. During his visit he shared a newly acquired bobblehead, Dr. Anthony Fauci. At the time he was serving as the head of the National Institute of Allergy and Infectious Diseases. It was cool looking, I must admit. I had him take a picture of me with it and immediately posted it on social media. I did not expect the reaction from some of my network, family, friends, and colleagues when they saw my post. The comments ranged from similar reactions to mine but also reactions from people who clearly were not fans of Dr. Fauci.

One reaction challenged me. I wanted to react quickly with a terse response. In that moment I reminded myself that I needed to practice a posture of cultural humility. I wrote them privately with questions that demonstrated curiosity instead of sending a terse response, including "help me understand" and "say more." I also shared that I wanted to learn more about where the other person was coming from.

I took this approach in a private messenger conversation and did not make the conversation public. This created a safe space for the conversation to happen. The term *safe space* refers to a space for a conversation to happen where people feel like they can have an honest conversation. I need to share here that a safe space, to me, does not mean a comfortable space. A lot of discomfort comes with having hard conversations. I left that conversation with a better understanding of where the other person was coming from. We ultimately did not come to an agreement, but we both left the conversation learning something new about each other. Also, our conversation was honest and friendly. If I had responded with a terse comment in a public forum, this could have led to a downward spiral of many people becoming angry or upset, perhaps typing responses (and responses to the responses) that would only deepen the divide and potentially harm relationships.

I encourage you to think about recent conversations you have had where a posture of cultural humility would have been helpful to gain a better understanding of the other person's point of view. What would have been different? Would the outcome have been different if you did? By taking the time to do this now, it will help you approach similar conversations in the future differently.

In March 2023, *The Wall Street Journal* published an opinion article by its editorial board titled "The Tyranny of the DEI Bureaucracy."[52] The editorial was critical of the way administrators at Stanford Law School had handled students who shouted down an invited speaker who had an opposing view and claimed DEI (now generally known as DEIB) has become a threat to free speech.

This article spurred an enlightening discussion between Lily Zheng, author and leading DEIB expert, and a businessman on a flight. On their social media platform Zheng noted that an older White man sitting next to them on the plane had just finished reading this article. Zheng asked his thoughts on it. He replied that the article made some good points, then turned to Zheng and said, "Why do you ask?"

Zheng explained that diversity, equity, inclusion, and belonging is their industry, which is in the crosshairs right now. The businessman put down the article, thought for a moment, and, to his credit, began asking questions from a place of curiosity. His first question: "What is the goal of DEIB?"

Zheng explained that the goal is to end discrimination and "build workplaces that work for everybody." They followed with this example: Approximately 14 percent of the US population is Black, and perhaps 14 percent of a company's applicants are Black, but only 8 percent get hired. Zheng pointed out that this discrepancy was problematic, and the businessman nodded in agreement.

Zheng continued: If 8 percent of that company's employees are Black, but only 4 percent stay for more than six months, then there is a retention problem—the company is not retaining its Black team members. Another nod. Zheng concluded this example with a final point: If 4 percent of the company's Black employees are still working there after six months but 0 percent make it to management positions, then that is also a problem. A final nod.

Zheng explained that DEIB is about finding and fixing the root causes of inequity and potential discrimination. The range of explanations could include biased policies, the lack of process, inadequate managerial training, accidental exclusion, or even intentional and overt racism. The goal is to find the causes, address them, and build a workplace free from discrimination that works for everybody.

In their social media post, Zheng noted that the businessman looked thoughtful. He explained that he owns a company and that one of the employees is a new mother. The company created a lactation room so she could pump at work. "Is that DEIB?" he asked. Zheng replied yes—they are recognizing that employees have different needs, they are working to meet those needs, and they are removing barriers that employees might face.

As these two strangers concluded their conversation, they agreed on two points: DEIB is common sense, and it is responsible business practice.

The purpose of sharing these examples is to show what cultural humility can look like in action. These conversations can be uncomfortable, but are necessary so you can start practicing cultural humility. The conversation I had over private messages about Dr. Fauci was not easy, but I left that conversation having a better understanding of what that person believed. I did not end up changing his mind about Dr. Fauci, but I now have a better understanding of his views. I shared Zheng's conversation with the businessman so you can be aware that conversations like this can happen in the most unlikely places. Be ready when an opportunity arises to practice cultural humility so you can hopefully help someone gain awareness of their views, not to change their minds, but to hopefully create an "aha moment" that causes them to think differently about something. You may also leave the conversation learning something new. You will need to remind yourself about the work you have already done in developing a growth mindset, staying curious, and listening deeply. These traits will help you engage in these types of conversations.

In Chapter 3 I shared how having a posture of cultural humility helped me accept my kid's newly identified gender identity. In addition, the posture has helped me approach challenging conversations about topics such as politics and faith. In using a growth mindset, I see these conversations as opportunities to learn. I approach them with a curiosity that allows me to remain as objective as possible. By asking questions, I have been able to gain an understanding of the other person's point of view.

I am seeking to understand and not to convince!

A caveat is that if you do not feel safe having a conversation with someone, then do not engage in that conversation. Not feeling safe could include a conversation with someone who may become angry and possibly violent, who is your superior and may threaten your job security, or who makes you feel uncomfortable in any way.

Our society would be in a better place if we all practiced having a posture of cultural humility in our conversations relating to a difference of opinion. We would leave conversations with a better understanding of others and leave people with a better understanding of us. This was the case in the story I shared in Chapter 2 when I was invited to be a panelist for the class. When you and other leaders have a posture of cultural humility, your organization will begin to look different, feel different to your talent, and everyone will approach challenges differently. Let me share what this can look like.

The Impact on Your Organization

In Chapter 4 I described what psychological safety looks like. It encompasses four areas: learner safety, challenger safety, collaborator safety, and inclusion safety. Organizations that practice inclusion and have a sense of belonging will be able to foster and encourage psychological safety. They will continually assess if their organization encourages psychological safety. As I shared in Chapter 6, this could be done by conducting an organizational climate study, where you ask your talent if they are experiencing psychological safety. If you determine that your organization is not fostering a sense of belonging or encouraging psychological safety, then you will need to develop an intervention plan so you can get better at this. Recent studies have shown that organizations that are not doing a good job at this lose talent at a higher rate, which translates to organizations not meeting their business objectives. If your organization is doing this well, it will mean your talent feels comfortable taking risks, they have a level of trust in their leaders and in each other, and there is a willingness to fail without fear of retribution.

In their book *Did That Just Happen?! Beyond "Diversity"—Creating Sustainable and Inclusive Organizations*, authors Stephanie Pinder-Amakar and Lauren Wadsworth share a process to use when an organization finds itself in a scenario involving an action it took that had negative consequences. Recall the examples I shared in Chapter 2 about the situations that Barnes & Noble and Walmart created for themselves. Organizations could benefit from using this process in those types of situations. That process is: retract, reflect, retrain, and re-approach.

- The first step is retracting. The organization apologizes as soon as possible with a posture of cultural humility; the organization owns the mistake.

- The second step is reflecting. This is where the organization takes steps to understand what happened and the origins of the mistake.

- The third is retraining. In this step, the organization may hire an outside consultant to help the organization evaluate what happened and determine steps it can take to ensure the mistake does not occur again.

- The fourth and final step is re-approaching the initiative. In this step, the organization can come back to the intent it originally had with the program or campaign. In the case of Walmart, it could look at what it meant by recognizing Juneteenth and the outcome the company desired to achieve. The organization has an opportunity to re-approach or revisit the initiative.

Even if you are making good progress creating an inclusive organization with a sense of belonging, your organization may still make mistakes like the ones made by Barnes & Noble and Walmart. The key is to have a process in place to help guide your organization when instances arise so you utilize a posture of cultural humility. Your organization may have an intention that is genuine, but the impact of a decision it makes has negative consequences, and it will need to be addressed. Having a plan and training your talent on how to approach situations that require a response, particularly those that may damage the psychological safety and the sense of belonging you want to create, will be vital.

The goal is to work toward minimizing the likelihood of those types of mistakes occurring and having a plan when they do happen. As with anything else when it comes to changing organizational culture, you will need to make sure new talent understands your organization's values, and you help them acquire the DEIB skills that will be necessary to keep your organization moving forward. This will require you to review your onboarding process. You want to provide continuous learning and development that is aligned with the indicators and initiatives you have identified within the dimensions of training and development.

The Impact on Your Community

I would now like to discuss what a posture of cultural humility can look like in your community. As I have shared, developing a posture of cultural humility will provide you with an ability to engage in conversations in your community that may have been previously difficult for you because of an inclination to want to convince rather than understand. Close your eyes and imagine a conversation you had recently that turned contentious with a neighbor, family member, a member of your congregation, volunteer in an organization you are involved in, and so forth. Specifically, think of one related to DEIB, politics, or faith.

Do you have one? Now imagine what it would have looked like if you had used a posture of cultural humility. This would have included approaching the discussion with a growth mindset or seeing it as an opportunity to learn about someone's perspective. It would have meant when that person said something you disagreed with, instead of shutting down, walking away, or becoming argumentative you would instead ask the person something like, "Please clarify what you mean by that" or "Say more." After you would have heard their response, you could have followed up with another clarifying question like this: "Can I share my perspective on this topic?" The goal is to create a space where the other person feels comfortable sharing their thoughts about a contentious topic because they believe you are coming from a place of curiosity, wanting to know more, rather than a place of judgment.

If you engage more frequently with these types of conversations, they will get easier, and your level of discomfort will decrease over time. This will make you a better community member and an exceptional leader. These conversations will take place in your faith community, in your volunteer organizations, in your neighborhood, and with your immediate and extended family. By modeling a posture of cultural humility, our communities will become better places to live and work.

When my kid Jayden shared with us their newly identified gender identity, my wife and I engaged in a conversation when they got home from school. In the conversation, both my wife and I took a posture of cultural humility and asked questions so we could understand more about Jayden's experience and how we could support them. We still make mistakes, but we have created an environment in our home where mistakes are OK, and we can use them as learning opportunities to continue to understand Jayden's experience.

Remaining curious during hard conversations will not always be easy. Do not misunderstand me. They will be hard, but think about what you can learn from having these conversations. You will be a better leader in your organization and your community. You will be that exceptional leader I described in Chapter 2. Your organization will be more inclusive and have that sense of belonging you desire for people to experience when they show up to work. Your clients will see the difference and will become raving fans of your organization. The community your organization belongs to will aspire to do the same, and the community you live in and interact with will also be inclusive.

Take Action

➤ Take time now to reflect on the conversation you envisioned earlier in this chapter where having a posture of cultural humility would have been helpful to gain a better understanding of the other person's point of view. What would have been different? Would the outcome have been different if you did? Write that conversation down and spend time thinking about how conversations could look differently moving forward.

➤ Write down the answer to the following question: Does your organization have a plan to address situations that have a negative impact on the sense of belonging and psychological safety of your talent? If it does not, what will it take to develop a plan so when things happen you will be ready?

➤ Take time now to think of an upcoming conversation you will be having that may turn contentious with a neighbor, family member, member of your faith community, volunteer in an organization you are involved in, and so forth. Reflect on how this conversation will look different now that you know how to use a posture of cultural humility. Now share your reflections with someone.

CHAPTER 8

The Destination-Free Road to DEIB

I OPENED THE BOOK BY describing the beginning of my journey toward developing a posture of cultural humility. That moment for me was what transpired in 1992 after the verdicts were read for the White police officers involved in beating Rodney King while I was in college. That was a watershed moment for me. It was my onramp onto the road toward becoming an exceptional leader. It was the moment I realized I could be a bridge for people. I began to develop a posture of cultural humility that would be instrumental in becoming an exceptional leader.

As you have read this book, you may have identified the watershed moment for yourself that caused you to take the onramp onto the road toward developing a posture of cultural humility that will lead to being an exceptional leader. It was the impetus for you to pick up this book, aside from the provocative title. Perhaps it was something you experienced in your personal life with your children, spouse, or partner. It might have been an experience in the workplace where a member of your team called you out because you inadvertently said something offensive, or the eye-opening reason someone shared with you regarding why they were leaving your organization. Whatever that watershed moment was for you, you have taken the onramp onto the road toward developing the missing piece to becoming an exceptional leader—cultural humility—so you can lead exceptionally in creating the inclusive organization that has the sense of belonging you wish it to have.

This road you now find yourself traveling on does not have a destination. Leading exceptionally in the areas of diversity, equity, inclusion, and belonging (DEIB) will require you to get comfortable with being uncomfortable and with ambiguity. It is not a box to check, an "i" to dot, or a "t" to cross. This road will require you to journey with others, build a network, and work with others, just as the redwood trees work together to weather the storms and wind they encounter over time.

This road you are on will, at times, lead you to a chasm that may seem impossible for you to cross. Behind you on that road is what you have accomplished on your journey in yourself, your organization, and your community. That chasm might represent a mistake you made that led to offending a group of people or something your organization did that created a social media frenzy. It could also represent something that happened in your faith community that led to controversy. With any of these examples you know you need to get to the other side and lead through what appears to be a very complex problem. Cultural humility is the posture or bridge that will help you lead through the complexity of diversity, equity, inclusion, and belonging efforts to get to the other side of the chasm.

Building a bridge requires a lot of work. It requires developing a plan that will enable you to build a bridge that will not fail under pressure. Having people who will provide expertise and support you will be key—perhaps a coach or consultant who can lend their expertise to help you develop that posture of cultural humility and construct that well-built bridge. After reading this book and completing the exercises in the Take Action sections, you are ready to build that bridge.

I now want to recap what we have covered to support you on your journey to develop and sustain a posture of cultural humility. This summary is a road map to continue in your development of becoming an exceptional leader so you can lead diversity, equity, inclusion, and belonging efforts in your organization and community at large.

The Road Traveled

Our journey together began with me sharing the three components that comprise cultural humility. These three components can be compared to the blueprint of the bridge you desire to become. The first is self-awareness and self-critique, which relates to the individual or personal part of developing cultural humility. The second is to begin to redress the power imbalances that reside in your organization. This has to do with the external impact of cultural humility. The third is changing the systems to be more inclusive. This translates to the systemic change that is needed so your organization can be more inclusive and have the sense of belonging you desire it to have. Another way to think about this is that developing a posture of cultural humility starts with you. It then moves to the organization and then, finally, to the community, which is comprised of the community your organization resides in and the communities you belong to (faith, volunteer, schools, and so forth). See Figure 6.

Figure 6. Journey Toward Cultural Humility

Cultural humility is important for you to be the exceptional leader you desire to be. It's not enough to be an effective leader when it comes to leading DEIB efforts. We are in a moment in history that requires exceptional leadership for our society to get better. Racism, bias, stereotyping, and violence against minoritized groups will continue to happen. Our society needs leaders to be exceptional, and that requires cultural humility. You can be that leader. If your organization is going to become more inclusive and have the sense of belonging it desires so that your talent stays and your clients or customers remain committed, then cultural humility is the posture you will need to develop as a leader.

I also shared the four components of psychological safety: learner safety, challenger safety, collaborator safety, and inclusion safety. I stressed the importance of cultivating a culture that creates psychological safety. This will be key in retaining your talent and for your organization to develop a posture of cultural humility.

I've shared three things you will need in order to develop a posture of cultural humility. They are a growth mindset, an ability to listen, and developing your curiosity. These are key to paving the road from cultural competency to cultural humility. Developing these three traits will be essential to your journey. If you have not completed the exercises in Chapter 4, I encourage you to start them, because they are foundational.

I stressed the importance of identifying the biases that exist within you so you can begin to do the work necessary to move toward developing a posture of cultural humility. I also touched on the importance of becoming culturally self-aware, which includes identifying the identities that are salient for you. I described the importance of becoming more aware of others around you, particularly those whom you lead or are in your circle of friends. I would like to highlight the iceberg exercise here. The key is to identify what it will take to lower the waterline for yourself and others. I ended by providing you with tools that will help you navigate the complexity of leading exceptionally when it comes to DEIB and reminding you of the importance of doing this work in community with others.

I stressed the importance of redressing the power imbalances that exist in your organization that you discover as you do the work of becoming more self-aware and developing other awareness. In developing other awareness, you will learn about others' lived experiences and begin to see the imbalances that exist in your organization. This will lead you to identify ways to redress those imbalances. I also described the characteristics of organizations that keep them from developing the sense of belonging they wish to create as well as offered ideas your organization can do to address those characteristics. I ended by stressing the importance of linking your DEIB efforts to your organization's mission, vision, and values. I also provided you with organizational examples, so you can see what that looks like.

I've shared the importance of having a framework to guide your organizational efforts to become more inclusive and develop a sense of belonging. The Dimensions of Diversity framework comprises four dimensions: organizational vitality and viability, recruitment and engagement, training and development, and organizational climate and intergroup relations. It requires you and your organization to identify the indicators you will use to determine if you are making progress. I presented ideas for potential indicators as well as examples of initiatives that your organization may want to undertake.

I described what cultural humility will look like for you as an individual and how conversations would look different if you approached them using a posture of cultural humility. I stressed the importance of remaining curious and what practicing curiosity looks like in the conversations you have with people on topics that you may have been hesitant to touch upon with people.

I then described what cultural humility would look like if an organization developed it, particularly as it relates to when organizations make mistakes that offend groups of people, such as the examples of Barnes & Noble and Walmart. I described a process an organization can utilize if things go awry. That process is: retract, reflect, retrain, and re-approach. I finished the chapter by describing the impact that practicing cultural humility would have on your community and how our society would ultimately be in a better place and would look very different than it does today. Perhaps we would not be as polarized as we are.

Now that you know what the road will look like, you have a road map, and you have begun to develop a posture of cultural humility, you are most likely noticing a change in yourself, perhaps starting with the way you engage in conversations about differences in perspective or controversial subjects that historically you have shied away from. Your leadership is beginning to look and feel different.

You are noticing that you are moving from being an effective leader to becoming an exceptional leader. Perhaps your team can begin to experience what belonging feels like.

They feel encouraged to speak up. They are taken seriously. The organization gives them space to be curious. They experience psychological safety and are not expected to be perfect. They feel welcomed and supported, and their contributions are genuinely recognized and appreciated. This leads to a strong desire to stay at the organization, and they can see themselves being a part of it for a long time.

As with any journey, you will encounter challenges that may deter you from staying on the road. You can and must push on so you can create an organization that will flourish in a way that will change people's lives—not only people in your organization but your families and your community.

At times, it will seem like you are struggling to get up that hill, but when you get to the peak you will see a beautiful sight. You will see people who feel included and have a sense of belonging. You will be that exceptional leader you want to be. And not only that—you will inspire others around you to develop a posture of culture humility to become the exceptional leaders you know they can be.

Take Action

> ➤ Now that you have completed this book, I encourage you to review your notes on all the previous exercises and determine your next steps. Perhaps it will mean finding a coach or consultant to create the space for reflection you will need to set goals for yourself so you can continue to develop a posture of cultural humility.

> ➤ Visit my website, www.DearWhiteLeader.com, and complete the cultural humility assessment so you can determine if you have a foundation to move from cultural competency to cultural humility.

> ➤ Share this book with others in your organization and your circle of influence. As a way to create community, you will need to provide accountability and support as you and others develop a posture of cultural humility.

"Be curious, not judgmental."
Ted Lasso

Endnotes

1 Janice Gassam Asare, "These Are the Reasons Why Your Black Employees Keep Quitting," *Forbes*, December 31, 2019.

2 Melanie Tervalon and Jann Murray Garcia, "Cultural Humility versus Cultural Competence: A Critical Distinction in Defining Physician Training Outcomes in Multicultural Education," *Journal of Health Care for the Poor and Underserved,* May 1998.

3 *Cambridge Dictionary Online*, s.v. "belonging," March 3, 2023.

4 Evan W. Carr et al., "The Value of Belonging at Work," *Harvard Business Review*, December 16, 2019.

5 Phyllis Weiss Haserot, "Use Backwards Thinking: Start with the B (Belonging)," (blog), You Can't Google It! (website), March 3, 2023.

6 Earl Fitzhugh et al., "It's Time for a New Approach to Racial Equity," McKinsey Institute for Black Economic Mobility, December 2, 2020.

7 Lily Zheng, *DEI Deconstructed: Your No-Nonsense Guide to Doing the Work and Doing It Right* (Oakland, CA: Berrett-Koehler Publishers, 2022).

8 Shaun Harper, "Where Is the $200 Billion Companies Promised after George Floyd's Murder?," *Forbes*, October 17, 2022.

9 Barnes & Noble (@BNBuzz), "Statement from Barnes & Noble," Twitter, February 5, 2020, 11:13 a.m.

10 Rachelle Hampton, "Why Barnes & Noble Swiftly Canceled Its 'Diverse' Book Covers for Black History Month," *Slate*, February 5, 2020.

11 Harper, "Where Is the $200 Billion?"

12 Pamela Newkirk, *Diversity, Inc.: The Failed Promise of a Billion-Dollar Business* (New York: Bold Type Books, 2019).

13 Stephanie Pinder-Amaker and Lauren Wadsworth, *Did That Just Happen?! Beyond "Diversity"—Creating Sustainable and Inclusive Organizations* (Boston, MA: Beacon Press, 2021).

14 Patrick Glynn, "17 Diversity in the Workplace Statistics Companies Need to Know," (blog), Insight Global, September 19, 2022.

15 Ibram X. Kendi, *Stamped from the Beginning: The Definitive History of Racist Ideas in America* (New York: Bold Type Books, 2016).

16 Richard Rothstein, *The Color of Law: A Forgotten History of How Our Government Segregated America*, reprint ed. (New York: Norton, 2018).

17 Wikipedia, s.v. "political polarization," last modified December 19, 2023, 20:08.

18 Amy Gallo, "What Is Psychological Safety?" *Harvard Business Review*, February 15, 2023.

19 Michael Gillespie and Kaitlyn Dyshkant, "Components of Psychological Safety: Inclusion Safety," *Medium*, June 18, 2020.

20 Ross Brooks, "Why Psychological Safety Is the Key to High Performing Teams," (blog), *Workday*, August 17, 2018.

21 Suzanna Windon, "What Is Cultural Competence and How to Develop It?" Penn State Extension, updated May 1, 2023.

22 Terry L. Cross et al., *Towards a Culturally Competent System of Care: A Monograph on Effective Services for Minority Children Who Are Severely Emotionally Disturbed*, (Washington, DC: CASSP Technical Assistance Center, Georgetown University Child Development Center, March 1989).

23 Carol Dweck, *Mindset: The New Psychology of Success* (New York: Random House, 2006).

24 Oscar Trimboli, *How to Listen: Discover the Hidden Key to Better Communication* (New York: Page Two, 2022).

25 Trimboli, *How to Listen*.

26 Trimboli, *How to Listen*.

27 *Cambridge Dictionary Online*, s.v. "bias," May 1, 2023.

28 "Bias," *Psychology Today* (website), December 10, 2023.

29 *Cambridge Dictionary Online*, s.v. "bias."

30 Mahzarin R. Banaji and Anthony J. Greenwald, *Blindspot: Hidden Biases of Good People*, (New York, NY: Bantam Books, 2016).

31 *Cambridge Dictionary Online*, s.v. "confirmation bias," May 1, 2023.

32 "The Circle of Trust," Hyper Island Toolbox (website), 2021.

33 "Intercultural Development Continuum," Intercultural Development Inventory (website), May 20, 2023.

34 Pabdoo, "Social Identity Wheel," University of Michigan (website), May 2, 2023.

35 Edward T. Hall, *Beyond Culture* (New York: Anchor Books, 1977).

36 Jennifer Brown, *How to Be an Inclusive Leader: Your Role in Creating Cultures of Belonging Where Everyone Can Thrive*, 2nd ed. (Oakland, CA: Berrett-Koehler, 2022).

37 Shane McFeely and Ben Wigert, "This Fixable Problem Costs U.S. Businesses $1 Trillion," *Workplace*, Gallup, March 13, 2019.

38 Jennifer Garvey Berger and Carolyn Coughlin, *Unleash Your Complexity Genius: Growing Your Inner Capacity to Lead* (Redwood City, CA: Stanford University Press, 2022).

39 Lisa Feldman Barrett, *How Emotions Are Made: The Secret Life of the Brain*, reprint ed. (New York: Mariner Books, 2018).

40 Tema Okun, "White Supremacy Culture," downloadable from website, White Supremacy Culture, May 2021 (originally published in 1999).

41 https://www.gallup.com/workplace/247391/fixable-problem-costs -businesses-trillion.aspx

42 McFeely and Wigert, "This Fixable Problem."

43 "About Us," General Motors (website), May 6, 2023.

44 "About Us," Asana (website), May 6, 2023.

45 "Our Standards of Excellence," About Humana, Humana (website), last updated April 7, 2022.

46 Daryl G. Smith, *Diversity's Promise for Higher Education: Making It Work*, 3rd ed. (Baltimore, MD: Johns Hopkins University Press, 2020).

47 Smith, *Diversity's Promise.*

48 Siri Chilazi and Iris Bohnet, "How to Best Use Data to Meet Your DE&I Goals," *Harvard Business Review*, December 3, 2020.

49 Peter M. Senge, *The Fifth Discipline: The Art and Practice of the Learning Organization*, revised ed. (New York: Doubleday, 2006).

50 John P. Kotter, *Leading Change* (Brighton, MA: Harvard Business Review Press, 2012).

51 Aashish Pahwa, "Understanding the Innovation Adoption Lifecycle," Feedough (website), February 20, 2023.

52 "The Tyranny of the DEI Bureaucracy: Diversity, Equity and Inclusion Offices Become Weapons to Intimidate and Limit Speech," editorial, *The Wall Street Journal*, March 17, 2023.

About the Author

Dr. Joel Pérez is an executive and leadership coach, speaker, and consultant who is passionate about helping leaders and organizations achieve their goals and develop a posture of cultural humility, so they can have the impact and create the culture they desire.

Joel is owner of Apoyo Coaching and Consulting, LLC and a Professional Certified Coach with the International Coach Federation (ICF). He specializes in guiding leaders to successfully lead diversity, equity, inclusion, and belonging (DEIB) initiatives; career transitions; identity-conscious leadership coaching; and coaching professionals who want to develop their cultural humility.

He has a certification in the Myers-Briggs Type Indicator, is a Qualified Administrator for the Intercultural Development Inventory (IDI), is a Gallup Strengths Certified Coach, and is a certified coach through the Academy of Creative Coaching. Joel has over twenty years of experience in higher education, serving in various key leadership roles. He developed a course titled "Strategies to Develop Self-Awareness" on LinkedIn Learning.

Joel identifies as a Mexican American/Chicano cisgender male and is a first-generation college graduate. He earned his doctorate in higher education administration at Claremont Graduate University. He has been married for over twenty-seven years and has four children, and he enjoys cheering on the Los Angeles Dodgers and watching films.

Contact Dr. Joel Pérez at info@dearwhiteleader.com. Learn more at www.DearWhiteLeader.com.

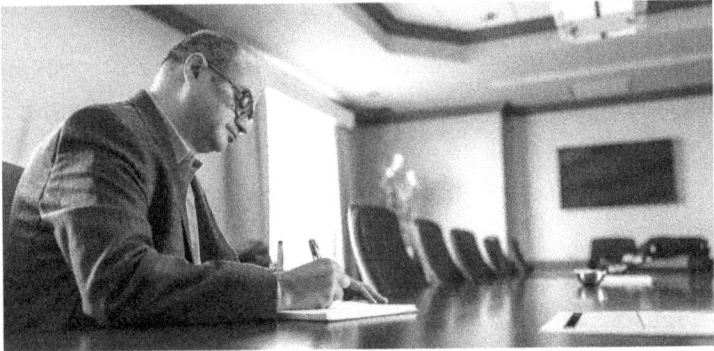

Bring *Dear White Leader* to Your Organization

If this book has spurred you to begin moving from cultural competency to cultural humility, I encourage you to continue reflecting on what you read. This is just the beginning. As I shared in the book, this is a lifelong journey that is filled with reward and meaning. You will be the exceptional leader you desire to become if you apply the principles laid out in this book.

If you are interested in having me speak on cultural humility at an upcoming event, facilitate a cultural humility workshop, guide your organization to move from performative statements to meaningful action, or create space for a one-on-one coaching engagement, you can reach me directly at **info@dearwhiteleader.com**. You can also find out more by visiting my website, **www.DearWhiteLeader.com**.

You can find all the Take Action exercises in this book at www. DearWhiteLeader.com under the Take Action tab, along with Apoyo Coaching's Cultural Humility Assessment.

I encourage you to share this book with others in your organization, your sphere of influence, and in your community.